CONFESSIONS

CONFESSIONS

John B. Cobb, Jr.

Concluding Chapter by
Bonnie Tarwater

PROCESS
CENTURY
PRESS
ANOKA, MINNESOTA 2023

Process Century Press
RiverHouse LLC
802 River Lane
Anoka, MN 55303

Process Century Press books are published in association with the International Process Network.

Cover: Susanna Mennicke

VOLUME X
THEOLOGICAL EXPLORATIONS SERIES
JEANYNE B. SLETTOM, GENERAL EDITOR

ISBN 978-1-940447-60-5
Printed in the United States of America

This series aims to explore the implications of Whiteheadian philosophy and theology for religious belief and practice. It also proposes that process religious thinkers, working from within many different traditions—Buddhist, Confucian, Christian, Hindu, Indigenous, Jewish, Muslim, and others—have unique insights pertinent to the critical issues of our day.

In 1976, we published a book, *Process Theology: An Introductory Exposition,* in which we aimed to "show the creative potentiality of a process perspective in theology." In addition to its explanation of process concepts and their application to Christian doctrine, the book noted the contribution of Whiteheadian thought toward "intercultural and interreligious understanding" and took an early stance on the ecological threat, claiming that process theology was prepared to "make a distinctive contribution" to this challenge.

Since the publication of that book, we have seen many others explore these and other themes in articles, books, and conferences. At the same time, the threat to planetary health and the need for "intercultural and interreligious understanding" has only accelerated. This series is an effort to support theologians and religious philosophers in their ongoing exposition of possible Whiteheadian solutions.

John B. Cobb, Jr.
David Ray Griffin

Table of Contents

Preface

This confession is by a disciple of Jesus. Jesus' message was directed to the particular situation of his day. He called his hearers to become his disciples. If enough had done so, then instead of violent revolutions against Rome, Jews would have treated Romans lovingly. The Jews would not have been expelled from their homeland. But most continued to support violent rebellion. Rome finally expelled them from Palestine. I am a disciple of Jesus because I find in his teaching the best guidance both for my personal life and also for responding to historical events.

Jesus has continued to call people to be his disciples all through the centuries. His twentieth-century disciples, Mahatma Gandhi and Martin Luther King, addressed themselves to very different situations. I am inspired by them. My intention is to address a still different situation, one that is more fully global.

My original intention was to write this manuscript primarily for myself. I felt that all my previous writings were written from the perspective of, or directed to, the church community, the theological community, the process community, or a particular organization. I did not state anything in those writings that I do not believe, but not everything that I believe came to expression. My personal priorities were not often clearly expressed.

Before I died, I wanted to write once to state, if only for myself, what I really felt most keenly about, without worrying about whom I might offend. That primary concern has, for many years, been the global crises and the policies of my own country that, on the whole, speed up the move to the destruction of civilization and the physical world that supports life. I have felt called by Jesus' Abba to do what I could for the healthy survival of the biosphere and for an ecological civilization for humans.

As I wrote, I noticed that sometimes, from day to day, there were changes in the global situation that required rethinking and rewriting. As long as I was writing for myself, that did not matter. However, some of those with whom I shared what I was doing persuaded me to share it more widely in the form of a pamphlet or even a book. That made it necessary to reduce the references to daily news. I deleted a lot. But the nature of my calling makes it impossible to separate my convictions from my judgments about what is currently happening.

While I was writing most of what this book contains, I, like you, was aware of the ongoing danger posed by the accumulation of nuclear weapons. But I had come to trust that the "mutually assured destruction" involved in a nuclear war would prevent any nation from initiating a nuclear war.

Quite recently I have learned that the United States has defenses that will probably prevent any enemy weapon from reaching the contiguous forty-eight states. I have connected that achievement with Biden's rhetoric and Putin's warning that if NATO goes too far in equipping Ukraine with the most powerful weapons, he will use nuclear weapons.

Biden has seemed to recognize that Putin may consider our equipping Ukraine with ultra-modern tanks as crossing the line. He resisted Ukraine's request for tanks. But he has set aside his doubts, even knowing that this may trigger Putin's nuclear response. Today's news is that both Germany and the United States will cross that line and arm Ukraine with these tanks.

This is frightening in itself, but its meaning goes farther. The decision-makers in the United States give higher priority to destroying Russia as a world power than to avoiding a nuclear war. If the tanks do not give Ukraine a sufficient advantage, other steps will follow. In the past, Putin has followed through on his warnings. Today, at this moment, the threat of nuclear war seems to me the most important topic to think and write about. My confessions would be different if I were writing them today.

Perhaps this acknowledgement will help readers to understand what fully developed process theology should be. There are truths about unchanging features of human life and God. They are important. But perhaps more important is to reflect on what is actually happening and how we should respond. I want to proceed with publication of an already outdated book. I hope it will encourage others to reflect on the new situation in which human beings seem unable to wait for the destruction of civilization by natural changes such as global warming. They may make it uninhabitable by human technology.

How could we resist this self-destructive planning? I answer the question as a disciple of Jesus. We would learn much from Gandhi and King. But we would look to Jesus for the deepest level of our response. That does not change because the danger of nuclear war has been pushed to the forefront.

The first six chapters below articulate commitments that I believe we individually and collectively need to gain from him.

There are then three chapters about my convictions that I find helpful, even essential, to bring about a new healthy civilization. I do not derive these aspects of my life and thought directly from Jesus. A disciple of Jesus is free to learn from any source. I think such sources help me understand Jesus and promote his teaching.

The next four chapters can be understood and appreciated by those who skip the previous three. They are efforts to help readers avoid being too easily persuaded by American propaganda and to offer deeper understandings of what is happening. It is in these chapters that the marginalization of the frightening movements toward nuclear war shows up. But this does not mean that what I have said there is now irrelevant or useless.

Bonnie Tarwater, a pastor who has served in both the Unitarian Universalist and UCC denominations, has much of the responsibility for my turning highly personal musings into a book. She grew up in a non-Christian, and even anti-Christian, home. When she finally heard the Christian message, she experienced it deeply as good news. She wants to share, but what she shares is emphatically a Christianity transformed by a woman's perspective.

Both of us think that if the church has a chance of giving life to the good news, it must be a transformed church. We agree that it is women who are responsible for the profound changes taking place, and that this is the most promising development in the church.

I wanted to conclude by noting the role of gender in Christian thinking and how a woman-transformed Christianity and discipleship to Jesus might give us new life. Thus the book ends with two chapters informed by gender. I wrote one on the history of gender in thinking about deity. I wanted to end with a chapter about whether women can save the church. That needed to be written by a woman. Bonnie wrote this chapter not only to answer that they can, but also to show something of what the transformed church will be like. My confession is that I believe the new leadership of women is our greatest hope, but I cannot personally describe the changes they can effect. So my confession ends with the future for which I hope, described by a woman.

During the course of writing, we tested the success of some of the chapters in communicating to other people. The results were discouraging. People do not want to hear the truth about the global situation and the depth of the needed changes. We decided that learning about these matters is profoundly disturbing to individuals. It is so threatening that our psyches defend themselves by shutting down.

We decided that, not just for the sake of healthy response to these chapters, but for the sake of absorbing the truth about what is happening and reflecting about needed responses, people need support. We thought that since the threats endanger everyone, groups might be formed to support one another in accepting the truth and seeking to respond wisely. The most practical proposal that came out of our work on this manuscript was to organize people in such mutual support groups.

Bonnie has worked extensively with small groups, and her concluding chapter introduces this proposal. She has also written an appendix with some advice about creating them.

If small support groups spread across the country, they would have a chance of affecting public opinion and bringing pressure to bear on those in power to choose actions that would lead toward sustainability and peace. Likely? No. But possible? Yes. If you are interested in this, it is not necessary to read the whole manuscript in order to become involved. I recommend reading the last chapter and the Appendix. You can contact Bonnie for further help.

1

Loving our Enemies

MUCH OF CHRISTIANITY has become a matter of believing
certain things about the results of Jesus' death on a cross.
Some of these theories assert that Jesus' death enables God to
forgive us and thus makes salvation possible for those who accept
these ideas. Those who hold that this is the gospel often have
little interest in what Jesus actually said and did as reported in
the gospels. What Jesus taught and revealed in his actions is
emphatically not a God who requires Jesus's suffering in order
to love and forgive us.

The Bible presents the story of Jesus as the "good news" or
"gospel," and it offers us four versions. It includes the story of very
early Christianity and some beautiful and deeply wise early Christian
letters, mostly by Paul. None of this is intended by the writers
to minimize the importance of Jesus' life. On the contrary, it is

intended to show that, although Jesus failed to end the movement of most Jews toward self-destruction, his teaching remains profoundly valuable for both Jews and Gentiles. In my view, the shift from the New Testament's attention to Jesus' life and teaching to a fantastic view of God requiring that his son suffer and die, is the emergence of a new, and quite unattractive, religion. My interest is in being a disciple of Jesus, not in persuading God to take Jesus' sacrifice as grounds for forgiving me.

Jesus was a Jew and had no intention of encouraging his disciples to be anything else. Individual Jews had their individual ideas about what Jews were called to be and do. And, of course, most Jews fell short of fulfilling what they thought of as "the law." Still, many truly and faithfully tried.

Most Jews believed that the heart of the law was the command to love God wholeheartedly and to love one's neighbor as oneself. Jesus fully agreed. However, he thought many Jews did not grasp the full meaning of this teaching.

First, there is the question of what "love" means here. In our day "love" often has sexual connotations. Obviously, that is not relevant to love of all neighbors. Some think of "love" as meaning "like very much." That also is irrelevant. The Bible is not asking that we like all our neighbors. We should "love" them whether we "like" them or not.

Some people argue that what is called for has nothing to do with feelings. We are called, they think, not to harm our neighbors but instead to act for their wellbeing. But at least in Jesus' case, there is a strong emphasis on motivation. We would not fulfil the call to love if we acted well out of fear of punishment or even simply from duty.

My understanding is that Jews, or at least some Jews, including Jesus, think that love is wanting the good for the other as we want the good for ourselves. The other is a human being with feelings and fears and hopes. We are to recognize that and support the other in connection with that. Whether we like the other person or not, we are called to want good for her or him.

Second, the question with which Jesus dealt at length is: Who are our neighbors? In Jesus' day and in ours, many think that our neighbors are people much like ourselves. Practically speaking, for many Jews in Jesus' day, the command to love one's neighbors was a command to love all Jews.

Jesus was clear that the "neighbors" we should love as we love ourselves were not limited to Jews. One of his best-known parables is about how a non-Jew, a Samaritan, played the role of neighbor to a Jew in great need. He depicted leading Jews as failing to help him. Clearly the Samaritan was a far better neighbor that these Jews. Jesus expected his Jewish hearers to understand and agree.

But Jesus went much further. And, in this point, he understood himself to break new ground. That did not mean that he thought his teaching was not Jewish. Probably he thought what he asserted was implicit in the call to love God. But he thought that Judaism had not yet made this point clearly. He was calling for Jews to follow him into a new understanding of what God calls us to be and do.

I encourage you to read the Sermon on the Mount, and especially Chapter 5 of Matthew's gospel. I quote here from the final paragraph of the chapter, but the full force of what I read can be felt only as it culminates the chapter.

> You have heard that they were told, you must love your neighbor and hate your enemy. But I tell you, love your enemies and pray for your persecutors so that you may show yourselves to be true sons of your Father in heaven, for he makes his sun to shine on bad and good alike and makes the rain to fall on the upright and wrongdoers. For if you love only those who love you, what reward can you expect? Do not the very tax-collectors do that?

Jesus words this teaching of love of enemies so as to apply to everyone at all times. However, he was talking to the Jews of his day as one who was offering them a path to liberation. Their enemies and persecutors were the Romans. They typically admired those who rose militarily against Rome out of devotion to God and the Jewish people. To begin his messianic ministry with the call to love the Romans says a lot about how Jesus called the Jews to adopt a new spirituality and lifestyle.

We may ask: What did it mean to love the Romans? Immediately before this passage Jesus gives an example. "If anyone forces you to go one mile, go two miles with him." That has little meaning for us, but it refers to the fact that a Roman soldier, who sometimes had to carry a heavy load a long distance, was allowed to force a civilian to carry the load for a mile. Jesus says, carry it for the soldier for a second mile. But the action by itself would not suffice. One must love the soldier as one loves oneself. One must be interested in him as a person. One must understand his suffering and joys. One may or may not like him. But one will care for him either way and be glad to reduce his burden.

Jesus thought that dealing with Roman oppression in this way would transform it. Most of these soldiers were themselves treated somewhat abusively by their superiors, and probably even by other soldiers of the same rank. Most of them experienced very little love. Being able to compel service from a despised Jew, no doubt, not only relieved them from painful work but also gave them some assurance that they too had some status, some power. One who is often treated with contempt may enjoy feeling contempt for those still lower down.

For that soldier to find that this Jew, whom he was enjoying exploiting, instead of hating him, cared for him as a person would certainly have been confusing. The soldier may not allow himself to believe he is loved during the first mile, but the second mile will make it difficult to remain unmoved. The soldier will feel understood and accepted. Hatred and contempt are gone.

The Romans knew that the Jews hated them and had repeatedly risen against them only to be crushed. The Roman reaction was to hate the Jews and feel contempt for them. Probably many Romans felt some satisfaction in making life difficult for Jews. The "second mile" and other expressions of Jewish love for Romans could change that. Love would probably not lead to political independence. But much oppression and repression could end.

Some Jews have, indeed, extended love to all and witnessed to that possibility throughout history. A Jewish minority has contributed to the American conscience disproportionately. Still, we can correctly say that the Jews as a whole did not follow Jesus in this way. They continued to seek liberation through violence. The Romans eventually drove them all into exile. Except for the first few centuries, for many of them, that exile was in countries dominated by Christians. As minorities, often mistreated, they actually followed Jesus' teaching more than the Christians. They have often held the United States to high standards of justice.

I grew up with high expectations of Jews in general. I expected them to be, as a group, more faithful to biblical teaching than Christians as a whole. Christianity in any culture was a mixture of biblical thinking with something else, something that often weakened and even corrupted the original teaching. I considered what has been called "orthodoxy" an example. The Bible opposes deifying any creature, including any human being. Christians made the break with Jews complete when they deified Jesus.

You will gather from this book that I greatly admire the thirty-year-old Jew whose teaching was miraculously profound. Indeed, just because I admire him so much, I strongly oppose turning him into an idol. I side with the Jews. Further, the biblical teaching of justice in no way depended on Jesus. I believed the Jews understood and followed their teaching more purely than Christians. When, after two millennia, they had their own country, I had high hopes that they would show us how we should deal with the inhabitants of a country we come to control. Perhaps they would go to great lengths to compensate the inhabitants of the land they conquered for what was taken from them. I thought they might go the second mile.

I was deeply disappointed. Regrettably, they have acted in much the same way Christian countries have acted through the centuries. Just as American Christians failed to love the indigenous people and Black Africans, and sometimes the Jews as well, Jews have failed to love the Palestinians in Israel or the Arab nations that opposed them. They have loved their "neighbors," the other Jews, far more impressively than Christians have usually loved Christians in other countries. But their national treatment of the Palestinians shows little concern for justice, much less for love.

Of course, evaluating Jews by Jesus' standards is hardly justified. Jews have never claimed to follow Jesus. But I thought that Jesus exaggerated when he implied that Jewish teaching was to hate their enemies. It has seemed that Jesus was right.

Still, it is Christians whose failure to love our enemies, or even advocate for love of enemies, is acutely disappointing. Jewish hatred of Romans led to their eviction from Palestine. Today, American hatred of Russians and Chinese is likely to lead to billions of deaths or perhaps an oppressive and hated global empire unable to steer a course away from ecological cataclysm. I fear we cannot count on contemporary American Christians for serious advocacy of the love of enemies apart from which our future is bleak indeed.

As I write, American newspapers continue to demonize Putin. President Biden knows that, according to diplomatic protocol, there are limits to what the leader of one nation should say about the leader of another with whom his nation is not officially at war. But it seems that his hatred of Putin is so great that he cannot control himself. His words increase the danger of a nuclear war. American propaganda has succeeded in making the great majority of Americans feel justified in hating Putin. I have not noticed any less hatred among Christians than among other Americans.

How would love of Putin as a fellow human being express itself? Would it mean that we would support him? What about our love for the Ukrainians who are suffering at the hands of Putin's soldiers? Clearly to love everyone cannot mean we agree with everyone or even that we fail to condemn the crimes of all. Indeed, we are called to evaluate as accurately as possible.

But those who follow Jesus' teaching would not demonize anyone. They would listen to Putin and try to understand him. The demonizing propaganda tells us that there is nothing to understand except that Putin is vicious and crazy and wants to expand Russian empire into all of Europe. But the evidence that he is vicious and crazy is based on our assumption that he is not telling the truth. Failure to love Putin means that we have no interest in hearing how he sees the situation. Our government makes sure that we do not learn how Putin thinks by preventing Americans from listening to Russian news.

In later chapters I will offer my views about Putin's invasion of Ukraine. In this chapter, I am not asking who is most responsible for the war. My point is that if we do not demonize our enemy, we will discover that the enemy also has a story to tell. If we love Putin, we will listen to his story.

Before the war, Ukraine at times engaged in the kind of negotiations with Russia that might have prevented it. But the United States discouraged it from doing so. After the invasion, there were negotiations. Again, the United States discouraged them. In the late summer of 2022, Ukraine and Russia nearly came to an agreement. The British prime minister, Boris Johnson, visited Kiev to oppose ending the war. The longer peace is postponed, the less willing is the Russian-speaking part of Ukraine to be ruled by Russian-hating Ukrainians.

If Ukrainians loved Putin, they might still dislike him. But they would really try to understand him. They would probably come to believe that Russia does not want to control the Ukrainian parts of Ukraine. It wants the Ukrainians who live there to renounce the desire to provide the enemies of Russia with bases for nuclear weaponry close to the heart of Russia. It wants to prevent harm to Russian-speaking Ukrainians at the hands of Ukrainian-speaking Ukrainians. These aims are not a threat to most Ukrainians. Probably far fewer would have fled their homes in parts of Ukraine where danger of war is minimal.

Unfortunately, Americans have blocked and suppressed the kind of information that would be gained by open study of what Putin has said and how he has acted. American propaganda persuades people that he is crazy and wicked and that nothing he says is to be believed. Instead, we are to believe that he wants to conquer and kill Ukrainians and that he is a threat to all Russia's neighbors. To love Putin is to understand him and to base responses on his real opinions and intentions.

To love Putin is to place his actions in a historical context. An American-supported coup, in 2014, toppled a government trusted by Russia and put the nationalist Ukrainians, including self-defined Nazis, in charge. Up until that time Ukraine was a bilingual country like Canada. The new government discontinued Russian as an official language. Russian Ukrainians saw that they would be second-class citizens in a country that hated them. Putin did not want to abandon his friends in Eastern Ukraine.

Would understanding Putin's goals have prevented the war or kept it very short? We will never know. But the chances for peace would have been much better than when truly frightening goals were projected on him as part of the demonizing propaganda.

In summary, loving enemies means seeking to understand them. Understanding enemies makes possible a more accurate view of what is happening. One can negotiate better with enemies if one fundamentally respects them as human beings.

If we Americans love both Russia and Ukraine, peace will come sooner and both nations can recover. There will still be unnecessary losses. But they can be ended sooner.

An historical example of the difference that love of enemy would have made is the ending of World War II in Japan. This is quite personal for me. I was a soldier in World War II. And near the end of my service, I was in the Army of occupation of Japan. I am proud of the American role in reconstruction under General MacArthur, but for me, there is an ugly blot on the United States' record with respect to the atomic bombs.

American culpability might be greatly lessened if the bombs had been needed to get Japan to surrender. But they were not. The Japanese were already suing for peace. They clung to one condition, extremely important to Japanese, trivial for us. The condition was that we would commit to respecting the person of the emperor.

Let us suppose that we had loved our enemies, the Japanese. That love would have caused us to understand, perhaps even admire, the willingness of millions of Japanese to die in order that their emperor be respected. Respecting his person would have cost us nothing. Indeed, we ended up doing so. But we demanded that surrender be unconditional.

The nuclear bombing of Hiroshima achieved that goal. It motivated the emperor to escape from his palace and get to a radio station to surrender and thereby save more millions of his people from dying for him. The bombing of Nagasaki served no purpose.

Things would have been different if we had not dehumanized the "Japs." The deaths of a few hundreds of thousand Japs meant little to us. They were not really human beings like us. Humiliating them into unconditional surrender seemed worth any number of Japanese lives. And an extra bomb just for good measure was no problem.

I have illustrated the wisdom of loving enemies in a couple of cases. I think even a little love would help a lot. But today, I am surrounded by wonderful, loving Christians who buy the propaganda of hate and feel no compunctions about hating the Russians, or, at least, Putin.

We have had two millennia of reading Jesus' Sermon on the Mount and learning that he considered the call to love our enemies as his most distinctive teaching. We still hardly discuss this possibility. Jesus noted that the inherited teaching was to love neighbors and hate enemies. Despite Jesus' correction, this inherited teaching dominates the thinking of American Christians. In this respect, most American Christians agree with the parts of the scriptures that teach hatred. It is interesting to see how Jesus dealt with those aspects of the Scripture of his time.

On one occasion, Jesus was speaking at the synagogue in Nazareth, his hometown. He asked for the Isaiah scroll and read from it. (Luke 4:18–19.) "The spirit of the Lord is upon me, for he has consecrated me to preach the good news to the poor, he has sent me to announce to the prisoners their release and to the blind recovery of their sight, to set the downtrodden at liberty, to proclaim the year of the Lord's favor."

He is announcing his mission. But what we should notice here is that he stopped quoting in mid-sentence. In Isaiah 61, verse 1, the sentence continues "and the day of vengeance of our God." Those for whom the fulfilment will include the suffering of their enemies do not love their enemies.

In our broader history, there has been progress. We owe this to a Hindu who, as a Hindu, was open to learning from others. He was impressed by Jesus, and especially by what Jesus considered his most original teaching. We should love our enemies. Jesus was specifically calling on Jews to love the Romans. Mahatma Gandhi saw the analogy with Indians loving the British. Unlike the vast majority of Christians, Gandhi took Jesus' teaching seriously. He persuaded millions of Indians, both Hindu and Muslim, to follow Jesus. The British gave India its independence.

Martin Luther King, Jr. saw that if there was any progress in

White acceptance of Blacks as full human beings, it was very slow. He gave his life to dramatically speeding it up. And he chose to do so as a disciple of Jesus. So, he studied Gandhi. King's work has globally changed the way people think of race and racism. Everywhere, there have been changes in laws. The pressure to include Blacks and other minorities is so strong that there are now many positions for which a White male need not apply.

My home state, Georgia, is an example both of the change and of the vast resistance to the change. Even those who resist the change act very differently now than before King. A Black Democrat was elected to represent Georgia in the U.S. Senate. The Republican leadership is determined to remove him. To do so, they have put up another Black, a popular athlete. This makes it difficult to charge them with racism. Without the deep changes brought about by King's successful obedience to Jesus, one cannot imagine that Georgians went to the polls to decide which of two Blacks would represent them in the senate. Meanwhile a Black woman ran a serious campaign for governor.

I have lifted up Mahatma Gandhi and Martin Luther King as the greatest examples of positive achievements based on the love of enemies. They are also the greatest examples of positive achievement based on nonviolent resistance. As a result, there has been a tendency to identify the call for loving enemies and the call for nonviolence. I want to point out that Jesus' explicit call is for love of the enemy. He also points out that he who takes the sword will perish by the sword. He clearly favors nonviolence. But whereas he calls for love of enemy without qualification, his opposition to violence does not seem to be absolute. Turning over the tables of the money changers in the temple is "violent" to some degree.

If we all loved our enemies, the amount of violence in the world would be greatly reduced. I am not sure that it would disappear altogether. And in a world in which individuals are violently treated by others and communities are violently treated by many governments, I think it would not end. In South Africa, the Blacks gave up their strict rule against violence, and their victory seems to have depended on that compromise. To assert that a nation should not use violence in response to a violent attack might speed up the global victory of imperialism.

My topic in this chapter is not a defense of violence. But I am calling for love of the violent enemy even if violence is required. I am rejecting the suggestion that Jesus' primary interest was to find ways of nonviolently defeating the enemy. Walter Wink has brilliantly showed how Jesus' call for turning the other cheek, and giving even more clothing than claimed, and going the second mile could turn the tables on the enemy. The techniques might have this result quite apart from love of the enemy. But Jesus teaches these nonviolent responses to cruelty as expressions of love. It is interesting that they might work apart from love, but if they are taken as ways for hate to express itself victoriously, we are not following Gandhi or King, and certainly not Jesus.

As more and more people recognize the desperateness of the human situation, it may be that fewer will simply dismiss Jesus' teaching as unrealistic. His teaching was the only chance the Jews had of continuing to live in their homeland. It probably would have worked. But Jews, like people everywhere, strongly tend to hate their enemies.

As I will make clearer as we proceed, there are no changes now being internationally proposed that go far enough to prevent catastrophes in the global climate. The two nations that are most powerful, most able to develop an improved response, and currently the worst polluters, are China and the United States. Their cooperation is our only hope. But the United States treats China as its greatest enemy and makes the enmity explicit in its actions and in the way it explains its actions. Unless Americans love those it considers its worst enemies, there is little chance for enough cooperation to save the world. The Jews refused to love their enemies and Israel as a country ended. If Americans refuse to love our enemies, the future of humanity on the planet is at risk. Should not we Christians be in the lead in calling for such love? Sadly, we are not.

The immediate focus of Jesus' call to love enemies is political. This is clear from the close connection he made between loving enemies and praying for "persecutors." The term refers to actions by rulers. Clearly Jesus was calling the Jews to pray for Romans. However, the whole of Matthew's chapter 5 makes it clear that Jesus refers also to daily relations with personal friends and foes.

When we shift our attention from politics to personal relationships, we find far more Christians trying to follow Jesus. They have forgiven individuals who have mistreated them and continued to express love toward those who have wronged them. Without some love for those who treat us badly, human society would break down. The relation of American Blacks to Whites is for me a remarkable one. That from the White side it has been marked by abuse and cruelty of many forms is indisputable. One might expect that from the Black side it would be marked by hatred and vengefulness. Of course, such feelings have existed. But what strikes me as quite wonderful is that throughout centuries of cruelty, Black women have not only taken care of White children, but also have loved them.

My speculation is that Blacks understood Jesus much better than did Whites. They understood that hatred would consume and destroy them. They learned to love their persecutors and thus to retain their own humanity. That was already a form of resistance. When Martin Luther King called them to resist their enemies lovingly, they already understood.

There is hardly anyone who has never felt abused or unfairly treated by others, even by their closest friends. There are few children who do not sometimes feel anger toward their parents. If the anger settles into a hatred that destroys love, family life is ended.

We know that we need to love those who act, at times, as enemies.

In conclusion, I return to politics. The United States has a two-party system of government. During much of our history the two parties have been enemies on many matters. But most of the time, the two parties are united by their common commitment to the wellbeing of the nation. Along with feelings of intense disagreement and anger toward members of the other party, there has been a deep connection as fellow Americans. There has usually been some effort to understand one another and find common ground.

Today, this underlying mutual love is radically subordinated to mutual opposition. For many, the support of an idea or a person by the other party is sufficient reason to oppose it. Primary loyalty for many is not to the nation but to the party. We see what happens when love of enemy is absent. Democracy depends on it. Our democracy is threatened.

Many Americans realize this and are enraged by it. There is danger that sufficient love for the United States may not survive the growing alienation. Regrettably, members of both parties consider the other to bear the entire responsibility. Just as Americans read only American propaganda and are ignorant of how the world is viewed by others, so, Democrats read only Democratic propaganda, and the followers of Trump read only Trumpite propaganda.

If we Americans took Jesus' message even a little bit seriously, if Democrats read Republican propaganda with an open mind, and if Trumpites tried to understand Democrats, we might still have a chance.

2

Evidence Favors Jesus' Abba

WE BEGAN WITH the famous call to love our neighbors and went on to explain Jesus' focus on loving our enemies. But in the Jewish and Christian formulations, this follows the call to love God. Loving God in the wholehearted way the Bible calls for is a rare accomplishment. Not every view of God evokes love. Within Christian experience itself, there are many problems responding to this call.

But today there is a more fundamental problem. Especially in the last century and a half, thoughtful members of the modern world have found that there is no need to bring God into the discussion. Indeed, they note that this only confuses the explanation of things and misdirects thought and action. For many, honesty dictates atheism.

I should note that at the theoretical level one reason for positing the reality of God remained. For practical purposes most people believe that there are unactualized possibilities. Even before there were creatures with eyes, it was true that someday there could be the experience of colors. Where did this possibility exist? There must be a sphere of potentials in addition to the sphere of all that has taken place. It is hard to think of such a sphere existing without a mind that entertained these possibilities.

Those who denied God sometimes denied that unactualized potentials had any existence at all. Some said they came into existence out of nothing. Some just said that experience cannot include the actualization of any previously unactualized potential. That is, everything in experience derives from things already in existence. There is no radical novelty. Most people just assumed there is novelty and saw no need to explain how it is possible. This is metaphysics, and if God is only the answer to a metaphysical question, they are not interested. Leaving the question unanswered was the dominant position of those who rejected God.

If there is no God, then the call to love God makes no sense. Even people who are supportive of Jesus believe that on this fundamental point he was the child of an age that was simply ignorant of what we have learned, especially through modern science. Theism has become such an obstacle to the hearing of the gospel that a good many honest and earnest Christians call for its abandonment.

Some think that Christian teachings can be reformulated without introducing "God." I respect these efforts and appreciate their importance. When I learn how the God who is being rejected is understood, I often agree that "He" does not exist, and that we can be glad that this is so. For some years my closest theological friend was Tom Altizer, famous for writing that the gospel is that there is no God.

But our friendship was not based on agreement. I think that his atheism, and that of most thoughtful people, was a case of throwing the baby out with the bathwater. The God who is rejected is usually not the God Jesus called Abba. I try to go back from the creations of the later church to that different God. As Christians, I think we should begin the discussion of God's existence by focusing on what Jesus revealed to us in his life and teaching.

We should also recognize that Jesus shared the cosmology of his day. This did not shape his fundamental understanding of God, but of course it shaped his language. To be faithful to Jesus today is not to try to think just as he thought. Philosophy, but especially science, demands that we pay attention to much that was not dreamed of in Jesus' day.

On the other hand, Christians should not blindly believe everything that most scientists believe. We should ask where the scientific method works well and where it does not. We have reason to emphasize its limitations as well as its achievements. We should study carefully those who have knowledgably examined the assumptions of modern science and proposed improvements. We are fortunate that some scientists have contributed to the clarification of the limits of science and even proposed ways of improving or supplementing it.

In my opinion, and that of a good many others, the English mathematician/scientist, Alfred North Whitehead, has done the best job thus far in asking and answering questions that should be asked and answered by Christians before they reject the theism of Jesus. It is true that modern science assumes atheism. It also believes that purposes play no role. It believes that there are no values. If I had not studied Whitehead, I would probably have sided with those who struggled to find meaning in an atheistic version of the Christian faith or, more likely, given up Christianity altogether.

Whitehead thought that just because the scientific method is geared to a physical determinism does not mean that purposes play no role in the world, or that there is no real novelty. He offered a philosophy that explained the role of purpose and the reality of novelty. In the process, he affirmed God. He recognized that the

God he affirmed was more like the Abba of Jesus than the more common views of God that he rejected.

In this chapter, I am basically restating Whitehead's ideas with reference also to the increasing support they receive from developments in science. I believe that many people are becoming atheists because scientists favor atheism just when science demonstrates its inability to complete its task without acknowledging a role for God. I hope that by the end of this chapter these brief comments in explanation of its title will make sense to the reader, even be convincing.

One way that God has been imagined is as an omnipotent creator and ruler. This is often supposed to be "Christian," but it is certainly not biblical. The Hebrew scriptures emphasize human responsibility which is completely denied by the idea of an omnipotent God.

Actually, the idea of one entity having all the power is nonsense. To be at all is to have some power. If God has all the power, God is all there is. But power can only exist in a relation. If God has all the power, then God has no power. If God has no power, God does not exist. I can't imagine how there could be evidence in favor of such a reality or unreality.

I doubt that anyone has ever really believed in such a God. I grew up in the church, singing, "God Has no Hands but our Hands." Many Christians were taught that it is orthodox Christianity to suppose that we have no responsibility for what happens. This is one of the great tragedies of human history.

The idea that God is omnipotent is one major reason for rejecting Christianity and, specifically, what many think is "Christian" theism. Even though no one really believes that nothing besides God has any power, some do suppose that God could save their loved one and does not do so. Or God could liberate their country and fails to do so, and so on. It is important to make clear that there is no such power in the universe. If that denial makes me an atheist, I am a dedicated atheist. I think Jesus and Paul were also "atheists." That this is not what anyone should believe is made very clear by Tom Oord's bestselling book, *God Can't*.

In the centuries when the Bible was being written, few people doubted that there were spiritual powers. Most people thought they were numerous. They turned to different gods for different purposes. For some, they turned to political rulers, who (for example, the Roman emperors), were considered gods. The sun, the moon, and the planets were also frequently deified or closely associated with gods. These gods were thought of as very much like human beings except that they had much more power. Also, whereas we die, they were thought to be immortal.

The question "whether Gods exists" sometimes means, "are there immortal persons much more powerful than we are?" What we know about emperors and planets makes their deification in this sense very implausible. But that there are immortal persons more powerful than we are is an interesting possibility. In cultures informed by people of the Book, (that is the Jewish, Christian, or Islamic scriptures) we would be more likely to call them angels than gods. The question for us is more likely to mean, is there one immortal person who operates in the entire universe? In the Sistine Chapel, Michelangelo depicts such a person as a very large old male.

In my view, the answer is "No." To be a person is to be finite in ways that would make it very hard for me to consider "God" as a person. Persons have spatial location, and people who believe in God as a Person usually show their tendency to think this way. They ask God to be with them, or to come to them. Their dominant sense of God, like their dominant sense of other human beings, is of one who is primarily spatially separate, much like a human person. In ancient times, such a divine Person was thought to be "in Heaven." And Heaven was thought to be "above."

People in Israel thought in much these ways. Their earlier writings express a background in which there are multiple gods. They thought that one of these gods had saved them from slavery in Egypt and had made a covenant with them. They thought their commitment not to worship any other god was crucial. Out of this refusal to worship other gods developed the view that there are no other gods. The God who saved them from slavery was also the God who created heaven and earth. This God is personally related also with every individual.

The real question for the people of the book—Jews, Christians, and Muslims—is whether they were right. Is there a reality that acts in the course of history and also in the creation of all things and is interested in each of us individually? The great majority of Jewish, Christian, and Muslim worship assumes such a reality, and many worshippers feel that they interact with this reality.

Now, much of the Bible also images that reality as Michelangelo depicts it. But many, in all times, understand that the one who created and creates, who cares for us all and influences us all, is very different from a human being. What is considered "orthodox" in Christian theology carries this difference, I think, much too far. For example, it denies both that God has feelings, and and that God changes through interaction with creatures.

Those who make this move point out that what is usually called God in the West is one instance of being. More ultimate, they point out, is the being of which all beings are constituted. They call this "Being Itself." It is so different from the God of the People of the Book that it cannot even be said to "exist." It is hard to think of it as an object of devotion or loyalty. I follow Buddha in dissolving it, but even if I did not, I would not think it honest to claim it as a replacement for what the Bible calls God.

So much for the negative. Now, for why I believe in God, and specifically the Abba of Jesus. I believe that there is that throughout the entire universe that works creatively and persuasively in all things, cares for all things, and calls for all things to play their role in serving all things.

I think of this as a purposive and loving Spirit and call it "God," or the "Holy Spirit," partly because I think orienting our lives to this reality, to work with it and allow it to work in and through us, is of immense importance for us and for what happens on this endangered planet. I think that a great deal of the Bible understands reality and the meaning of human life in much this way. I think that this is clearest in Jesus.

There is lots of evidence for the reality of this God. It is supported by our personal experience. Moment by moment we experience ourselves as shaped by our personal past and by the whole past. But we do not experience ourselves as only and necessarily the passive outcome of the past. When we are that, it is because we allow ourselves to be that. We have a sense that there are other possibilities. And we have a sense that these other possibilities are not neutrally there. We feel that we could do better than we have done. And much of the time we know we are not being passively determined by the past. We are seizing emerging possibilities for the better. This all makes sense if a universal spirit is calling us forward without compelling us.

I have named this "the call forward," and I consider it existentially the greatest evidence of God. For me, it refutes the modern scientific worldview, which was based on the exclusion of purpose from any explanatory role. But I have also recognized that the congeniality of my description of my experience and my understanding of God might be because of the influence of my belief in God.

The description I offer of my experience, which I believe to be universal, is called "phenomenological." Perhaps the greatest phenomenologist of the second half of the twentieth century was Martin Heidegger. He was an emphatic atheist. In his most rigorous book, *Sein und Zeit (Being and Time)*, he wrote about *"der Ruf nach vor."* I found that what I had written about the call forward was not at all original. Heidegger had described it. That humbles me, but it also assures me that finding this phenomenon is not limited to those who want to find evidence of God.

We differed only in the explanation of its occurrence. I think the call comes from God. Heidegger denied the reality of God. His solution was to say that the call comes from ourselves. I think he might admit that, phenomenologically, it does not feel that way. This is an example of a metaphysical pre-commitment that forces an explanation that is otherwise less convincing. If one thought the reality of a purposive Spirit pervading the universe was possible, but wondered whether it existed, I believe that careful examination of our own experience would count as positive evidence.

Why are so many people committed to atheism? Partly, I think, the fault lies with the absurd and outrageous things that have been affirmed of God. Instead of carefully examining whether belief in God entails those characteristics that they rightly reject, they simply reject the whole topic.

However, this sheer rejection has its major starting point in the origins of modern science. The key thinkers who provided the intellectual context for modern science were impressed by the technological genius that went into the creation of clocks. We could say that clocks have the purpose of telling us the time. But if we ask why each part functions as it does, our answer will be in terms of mechanical causes. Aristotelian "final causes" or purposes play no role in the functioning of the clock. Modern science is the study of efficient causes. The efficient causes are found in contiguous physical entities. God has no place.

Again and again, scientists have been able to give purely physical explanations of phenomena previously thought to express God's purposes. For some time, God was allowed a role in creation, but evolutionary thinking largely ended that. Until humans were found to have evolved in much the same way as other species, science had accepted a dualism of the human and the natural. They did not doubt that humans had purposes.

But evolutionary theory ended that as well. The social, biological, and chemical sciences explained more and more of what had previously been left to the humanities. Even in regard to matters of faith and spirituality, the evidence seemed to grow that all could be explained without appeal to purpose. If purpose plays no role, then there is no purposive spirit in the universe.

Humanism did not disappear. The form that now had the most status was existentialism and the phenomenology it developed to describe human experience. It showed that we are not the zombies implied in the universalization of the scientific worldview. But, as children of the modern world, most existentialists and phenomenologists assumed atheism, or at least professed it in order to retain credibility in the university.

When I was studying in the University of Chicago in the late forties, the fact that God was totally absent from the explanation of everything in all the sciences and humanities led me to have my own "death-of-God" experience. If everything, including my own experience, was explained by all the authorities and experts without reference to God, it seemed that God played no role. There can be no evidence of a God who does nothing. My prayers bounced back from the ceiling. In spite of the fact that I had the great good fortune of studying with Charles Hartshorne, I was sucked into the Godless and purposeless modern world view.

That worldview still controls and censors. But it is crumbling. And the science that was its home has been undercutting it. Today, it is quite acceptable among scientists to admit that they have no explanation of consciousness and no scientific programs in sight that will change that situation. This means that science cannot encompass a very important part of the humanities.

The scientists of the 1940s recognized that quantum theory was a problem, but the vague assumption was that in time it could be assimilated. Now, however, its conflict with the dominant worldview is fully established, with no expectation that future findings

will help. Indeed, the evidence in many fields is increasingly difficult to fit into the still dominant worldview.

In this context, David Bohm could develop a quantum theory
far more congenial to Whitehead than to Newton. Few followed
him, but the tendency was to ignore and leave alone rather than
condemn and excommunicate. Rather than seek a coherent and
inclusive view of nature, each academic discipline is now allowed
to develop what theory it needs without much concern for how it
relates to other academic disciplines. However, the great exception
is that no appeal to a final cause or to God is allowed.

Even this is now challenged by the evidence. I have mentioned
in previous works that my own theism was temporarily crushed
by the overwhelming success of studies in every field, including
religion, to explain their data atheistically. But this is no longer
true of scientific cosmology.

Scientists have found that the universe is "fine-tuned" for life.
That means that, in many respects, where exact quantities and
relationships seem arbitrary, the ones that obtain turn out to be
the only ones that would have allowed for life. That the universe
could easily have been different in all these respects according to
scientific evidence is not disputed.

Scientists like to show that what happened had to happen. To
whatever extent possible they like to present the universe as something that can be explained entirely by efficient causes. However,
they are at times willing to accept that some things happen by
"chance." They make no effort to show that the fine-tuning can
be explained by necessity. So, they appeal to "chance." There are
mathematical accounts of chance. Of some occurrences there is a
chance in two. Of others, a chance in ten.

In the case of each instance of fine-tuning, the chance is much
less than one in ten. Every time another case of fine-tuning turns
up, the improbability takes a quantum leap. If this is all chance,
it is one chance in millions. If one approaches this now fully

acknowledged fact without presuppositions, the judgment would be that the fine-tuning of the universe is purposeful. The scientific evidence is that an aim at life pervades the universe.

I will not guess the personal views of individual scientists. Some may now allow that, after all, purpose may play an important role in the world. The other day I heard a lecture by an astronomer cosmologist. He told us he thought that life has probably developed at many times and places among the vast number of planets. He thought that wherever conditions allow, it would happen. In other words, practically speaking, he thinks that the universe favors life where it is possible. The dominant scientific physicalism disagrees. But he was hardly conscious of that. He thought that his scientific colleagues shared his belief that the universe favors life and improved forms of life. So far as I can see, this does not make them less scientific, unless one defines science as reductionist materialism.

Scientific reductionism has a sufficient hold on the scientific community that it seeks an alternative to allowing purposiveness a role. If there are or have been millions of universes, then they don't need to acknowledge that purpose plays a role. If there are or have been millions of universes, the fact that one of them favors life does not challenge the view that this is a matter of chance.

Of course, any theory of this kind would have to start by redefining "universe." It has meant "everything" or "all that is." One cannot have more than one "everything."

I am not aware of a careful study of the likelihood of other universes. I doubt the view that there are other universes concurrent with this one can be coherently formulated. More plausible, given the dominant theory of the big bang, is that what we have called the universe was preceded by something, and that we will define our universe as what began in the big bang. Then we can call what preceded the big bang "another universe" and hypothesize that it was governed by different laws. In infinite time there could be any number of universes, although there could also, so far as evidence is concerned, have been only one preceding the Big Bang. Also, all universes might be fine-tuned for life.

Much work is needed before we have a developed theory about the successive universes and how they help the atheistic cause. Obviously, if they also gave birth to life, the atheist cause would not be advanced. I think it would be weakened if what came before this one was extremely different from this one or if the development toward the support of life progressed in successive universes.

The big bang theory supports the multiverse theory by explaining the beginning of our universe in a way that allows for a predecessor. On the other hand, I am not aware of a theory of an end of our universe that suggests the birth of another. In order that the existence of other universes help to make the idea that all the fine-tuning was by chance, some possibility of a successor should be explained. I think the other universes would need to be like this one except in regard to those features that are fine-tuned to support life, but different in that respect. What would be the likelihood of that? (In the chapter on "Truth" I will explain that the whole big bang theory is highly doubtful.)

So, does the fine-tuning of our universe for life prove that there is purpose in our universe? No. But by far the simplest explanation is that an aim toward the realization of value pervades the universe. Indeed, it is the only explanation yet offered. The alternative is a suggestion that it might be possible to develop a theory that it is a matter of chance.

Very few of our most confident beliefs are "proved." I am confident that I live in a social world inhabited by other people who have their beliefs and feelings. Can I, or anyone else, "prove" that belief? Maybe, after all, there is an omnipotent being who controls our thoughts and memories and expectations in totally misleading ways.

Should I suspend belief that my purposes affect my actions because I cannot "prove" that this is so? No. Reason calls for us to believe what we confidently find to be our experience unless there are strong reasons not to do so. If the only reason not to do so is that many scientists are committed to a particular sixteenth-century metaphysics, reason indicates we should go with what we experience, not with their ungrounded faith.

It would be wonderful if scientists would ask about their proof of atheism. They would discover that they have none at all. It is true that for a long time they were able to extend their scientific explanations in more and more areas. Would it not be sensible to allow evidence of the sort they now have to tilt the scales? But of course, if you want very badly not to believe something, regardless of evidence, you can manage. Scientists were rightfully critical of Christians who clung to mistaken ideas despite the evidence. But it is now scientists who dogmatically affirm beliefs even when the evidence is against them. It would be a mistake for Christians to consider authoritative the scientists' extremely speculative beliefs on a topic they have not thought much about.

Alfred North Whitehead is the person whose writing about how God is experienced I most fully trust. I have dealt thus far with what he calls the primordial nature of God. It offers graded possibilities as lures toward a fuller personal life and one that contributes most to the life of the planet. It has lured the universe to make life physically possible.

Whitehead also introduces what he calls the consequent nature of God. His understanding is that each moment of our experience includes aspects of all that has happened. We are influenced by all that has occurred. This means that, in some tiny way, everything in the past participates in everything in the present.

The influence of others is primarily emotional, and most of it is unconscious. If we are in a group of angry people, our experience will be affected by their anger. Of course, the beliefs and opinions of others also shape our beliefs and opinions. This also means that my emotions, beliefs, and opinions influence others. Most of this inclusion and re-enaction of the experience of others is extremely partial. Most of what I feel and think is lost to me in the ongoing processes of history.

Whitehead proposes that the universal Spirit feels our experience with us and preserves it forever. Whatever we do, even what seems to have no effect in the world, contributes to the life of God. God knows us and understands us better than we know and understand ourselves.

Thus, God's love for us takes two main forms. The primordial nature of God lures the universe to constitute itself so as to make life possible. Where it is possible, then, this side of God lures entities into modes of being that over time become capable of rich intrinsic experiences. The emergence of life is a very important step. Then, at least with the emergence of human beings, the same lure becomes the call forward in ordinary human experience. The Consequent Nature of God accepts what we do and who we are with full understanding, endlessly forgiving, accepting, and loving every creature.

Is there any experiential evidence for the Consequent Nature of God? Yes, but certainly not a proof. When historians write about the past, they assume that there is something to write about. Its being past does not seem to mean that it has no reality anymore. We feel that statements about the past can be true or false even if we doubt that anyone will ever know. When I'm asked about a past event, I try to dredge up memories, but I often feel doubtful that they are accurate. That means I assume that there is truth about the event. The event still has just the features it had when it first happened.

In short, we feel that past events still are in some way what they were. Whitehead's meditation about the status of past events led him to the view that they are all still present in the divine "memory." I think that if you ask the question, you will find it hard to come up with a more plausible explanation.

There is also a pragmatic reason to believe. A group of Christians in England banded together in the Oxford Movement. They strengthened one another in their faith and encouraged others to do so. They also worked to help others. Perhaps their greatest contribution was their unique success in dealing with addicts, such as alcoholics. Alcoholics Anonymous developed out of their work.

They thought that belief in a "Higher Power" was of central importance in breaking the hold of addiction. Since that time, such belief characterizes fewer and fewer people. One might expect that Alcoholics Anonymous would evolve and go along with the modern world in dispensing with such old-fashioned ideas. But it has not. It is more interested in what works than in what is fashionable, and this pragmatic focus has worked in favor of retaining belief in a Higher Power.

I undertook this writing because I wanted a chance to share my beliefs without worrying about who might be offended by what. But as I conclude this section on Jesus' Abba, I realize that, while I do believe everything I have written here and elsewhere, the truth is that I believe more, and I should acknowledge that the "more" does not follow smoothly from what I have written. It is grounded in personal experience that is very important for me but has no claim on anyone else. In the interest of full disclosure, I will describe briefly an experience that belongs to the "more."

As a soldier in World War II, at one time, I was serving in the Pentagon and living in Washington. I was a pious youth and customarily knelt to pray by my bed before getting into it each night. One night, just after I knelt, I felt my context transformed. I heard nothing. I saw nothing. But I was surrounded and pervaded by a presence. In a way that I had not known to be possible before and have not experienced since, I felt totally loved, totally accepted, totally affirmed. I learned the meaning of "bliss." The bliss lasted, probably, only a minute or two. Then faded.

I can write with some detachment about God loving every

creature. I believe that. But my experience of being loved was not just the realization of that. It was more, much more. And I still cannot really understand how the Spirit that loves everything can also make itself felt so intensely and profoundly in an individual case. I almost left it out here, as so often, because I am so deeply shaped by our "nothing but" culture that I am almost embarrassed to admit that I have experienced much "more," and still can hardly believe it myself. Still, I am deeply, very deeply, grateful to Jesus' Abba.

3

Serving Abba and
Serving Money

I HAVE ARGUED that the evidence does not favor an almighty, wholly-controlling being, but it also fails to support the devaluation of purpose in the modern worldview. There is no need to decide between an omnipotent deity and a purposeless universe. The evidence of our own individual experience and of the entire life-enabling universe support the idea that there is a purposeful force or spirit that plays a role in all that happens but does not unilaterally decide anything. Jesus called it "Abba."

Israel's choice of that term says something about the popular understanding of deity there. It is, of course, the word for "father." As in other parts of the world, people often have a word for "father" coming from the sound a baby makes. I grew up calling my father "Papa." Of course, the Hebrew babies experienced their abbas as powerful. But more significant than power in the use of that term are intimacy and care. The primary relation between infant and father suggested by the term "Abba" is mutual love. That Jesus used this language just means that he felt comfortable with the basic understanding it expresses.

The older child may experience the father more as one who lays down the law and punishes failures to obey. Some Jews did think in these terms. Jesus did not. Most clearly in respect to God, he thought in terms of the spontaneous love of the baby. One might say that his teaching about God reenforced the connotations of calling God "Abba."

There is some basis for thinking this was important in the very early church. We learn that among the Greek-speaking Christians, when their experience of God was most personal and intimate, they called out "Abba." One passage in Paul's letter to the Romans makes that clear. It is clear also that this was not something that Paul taught his followers to do. It was spontaneous. "All who are guided by God's Spirit are God's sons. It is not a consciousness of servitude that has been imparted to you, to fill you with fear again, but the consciousness of being adopted as God's sons, which makes us cry 'Abba', that is, Father. The Spirit itself testifies with our spirits that we are God's children" (8:14–16).

Hence, I would claim that Jesus' use of the term "Abba," although fully explained by the culture in which he lived, had for him and for those who followed him a deep meaning.

For this reason, instead of simply saying Jesus' Father or Jesus' God, I say Jesus' Abba. Probably no detailed statements about exactly how Jesus thought of Abba can be derived from reliable texts, but that he thought of the relationship as deeply personal and intimate we can say with some confidence. Abba is the deity we are called to love and lovingly serve.

Jesus made clear that giving our devotion to Abba is costly. This costliness might be the sacrifice of one's own life, as in Jesus' own case. But Jesus did not encourage his hearers to get themselves killed. What specific kind of attitude and action does Jesus empha-size as indicating that one is properly devoted to Abba? What impresses me as Jesus' typical test of whether one is rightly oriented is one's relation to money.

On one occasion, an attractive young Jew who was wealthy, after telling Jesus that he obeyed all the laws, asked what more he needed to do. Jesus told him to give away his wealth and invited him to join the apostles. The man went away sorrowful, and Jesus also was disappointed. He commented: "It is easier for a camel to get through the eye of a needle than for a rich man to get into the Kingdom of God" (Mt 19:24).

This extreme statement does not correspond to the rest of Jesus' practice and teaching. Luke tells the story of another rich man, Zacchaeus, the principal tax collector in Jericho (Luke 19:8-9). He was so eager to see Jesus that he climbed a tree so as not to be blocked by the crowd. Jesus saw him and told him that he would spend the night in his home. Tax collectors as a group were hated, because so often in the process of collecting taxes for the govern-ment they also squeezed money from the masses to enrich them-selves. Many were shocked that Jesus would stay at the home of a notorious tax-collector. But Zacchaeus announced his repentance: "Master, I will give half my property to the poor, and if I have defrauded anyone of anything, I will repay him four times as much."

Jesus does not tell him to give away all his money. He is satis-fied that Zacchaeus is now serving God, not wealth. That sufficed. He says to Zacchaeus: "Salvation has come to this house today" (Luke 19:9). It was because he thought God was calling the rich young man to become one of the apostles and saw that his wealth prevented him, that he spoke so extremely about the rich.

Jesus' overall view of money is stated succinctly in the Sermon on the Mount. We cannot serve both God and money. We have to choose. Some Christians feel that once they have given a tithe to the church, they are free as Christians to seek riches for themselves.

As in so many instances, Jesus dismisses this kind of solution. There are no rules. What God will call someone to do is not ours to decide. But when the call comes, how does one decide? The rich young man chose money. The tax collector chose God.

The extreme response of Jesus to the decision of the young man, however, has more practical meaning. What does it mean to be rich in the midst of people suffering for lack of money? God's call is always to love one's neighbor. Can one continue to pile up money one does not need in the face of the needs of others? Jesus did not lay down rules for dealing with this situation. He only called for love of God and neighbor. But he had expectations, positive and negative, of what love would lead to. He was very doubtful that it would lead to accumulating unneeded money while others starved.

In early Christian times, outside of a few contexts such as the churches, wealth was honestly and openly sought. The idea that people are called to subordinate their interest in money to some other norm was hardly considered. A rich man was more likely to flaunt his wealth as a mark of his success and greatness than to suppose that he might need to give it away.

Does that sound familiar? For many centuries in so-called "Christian" countries, concern for the poor at least moderated the enthusiasm for riches. The rich sought ways to justify holding onto their wealth. In our secular day, the situation has largely returned to the dominant culture of Rome. Being rich is being successful. It is an ideal to be emulated. Jesus calls for a reversal of values.

What has actually been happening has been the increasing acceptance and affirmation of seeking one's own wealth as one's primary goal in life. This has affected all our institutions. Perhaps the change with regard to education is the most impressive victory of money.

When I went to college, I justified this expenditure of time and money by the belief that it would improve my ability to serve others. To be a good leader in the community, one needed to understand its history and appreciate its great achievements. By going to college, one would be able to pass on the best of the culture to future generations. One would also understand and appreciate such values as justice and help the community to implement them.

Of course, the explanation of why I went is in fact chiefly that in my family and among my friends it was taken for granted that, after one completed high school, one would go to college. And no doubt I also went in order to be a part of the professional middle class and enjoy its privileges. My point is not that noble ideals actually shaped my behavior. But the culture expected people to look in the direction of such ideals in making basic decisions about their lives.

What about now? Most students say that their purpose in coming to college is to get a better job. If we ask what makes a job better, we will almost always be told that it pays better. On the whole, colleges assume this is what students are concerned about, and so promote themselves accordingly.

The education they receive tends to confirm students' understanding that they are properly organizing their lives around the pursuit of money. The teaching in the economics department is clearest. The world is made up of competitive individuals. What they compete for is money. The rational thing to do is to learn how to compete successfully.

This message is not so explicit in other academic disciplines. But they all pride themselves in being value-free. Possession of values is viewed negatively. Money is taken for granted as something people want. The values that are downgraded are those that might distract from the wholehearted quest for money.

Most colleges called themselves "liberal arts" colleges. This is true even today. Most faculty members have received the requisite PhD studying an academic discipline. These disciplines aim to be value-free. With this depreciation of values in their training and in their guilds, those asked to teach liberal arts have difficulties.

Sometimes the subject matter is reorganized as an academic discipline. In many colleges these "humanities" have to work hard to maintain a foothold. Their contribution to the goal of getting a better job is questioned.

To be fair, colleges and universities have and affirm values with respect to student life outside the classroom. Many do a good job with their students. They encourage students to accept one another regardless of differences in race or sexual orientation. They usually push for full equality of women. In employment, they favor racial diversity. They encourage travel abroad so as to broaden the students' horizons. It would be absurd to say that universities are value-free.

Nevertheless, the curriculum matters. Many students in many colleges are not residential. The great things promoted by many colleges with residential students do not affect an increasing segment of the student bodies. Only the curriculum is considered essential for the degree that is needed for many good jobs.

We have recently been hearing of professors chaining or gluing themselves to buildings. This is academically acceptable if the professors do it on their own time. It should not affect their teaching. Some have spent time in prison because of their protests. Professors as a group may be above average in working for good causes. My objection, that professors are expected to teach academic disciplines that are value-free, is not at all a statement about the professors. The great mistake, from my perspective, is that they are asked to avoid introducing their own convictions and commitments into their teaching. An influential book is entitled *Save the World on Your Own Time*. Universities are not interested in teaching students that it would be good to save the world or how to go about it.

In spite of university norms, there have been two occasions on which faculties in particular disciplines became socially active. The first occasion was in the late sixties. Professors of "ecology" became alarmed about the speed with which natural ecologies were being destroyed by human activities. To this day, those who are concerned about the environment think of themselves as part of the "ecological movement." Then, in the early years of the new century, climatologists became deeply concerned about the prospects of a warming planet. "Climate change" or "global warming" became the center of environmental thinking and thus a focus for national governments. Climatologists are looked to for guidance by world leaders.

These enormous contributions of professors in two minor academic disciplines certainly give the lie to any charge of university irrelevance. We owe these faculty members a great debt. But they also indicate that if, fifty years ago, universities had organized research around giving guidance to society about questions of practical importance to us all, we might not be facing such frightening threats today.

Among the top twenty universities, Emory is one of the most resistant to giving up a concern for values. It belongs to the United Methodist Church. It boasts of its commitment to values. A few years ago, a retiring president wrote in its magazine how much he cared about communicating values to the succeeding generations. He described all sorts of things he had done to promote values among students. But he said that, of course, he understood this could not be done in the classroom. He cited the book I mentioned above, *Save the World on Your Own Time*, that scolds professors for introducing values into the classroom. They are paid to teach value-free disciplines. How great it would have been if Emory University had explicitly and publicly rejected the idea of complete separation of facts and values in the academy. Its Christian roots called for that, but its commitment to radically secular academic norms was stronger.

As people become desperate in face of environmental decay and impending catastrophes, many wonder why the educational community remains so aloof, and this question has registered inside that community as well. Many examples of important changes can be found. I mention one that comes from the heart of the academic community, the American Academy of Arts and Sciences.

In its official publication there was a public announcement of a change in policy. In the past, they noted, they had understood the academy's task to be to provide the world with factual information. How that information was used was not its concern. It was available to those who had the money to support the educational institutions. Mainly this was large businesses and the governments that worked with them. However, when climate change threatens society as seriously as now, the academy should respond by developing its own analysis and shaping its research directly to deal with this pressing need.

This is presented as an emergency measure. It is not a change in the understanding of the university's proper mission. It does not suggest that curricula might be redesigned so as to be relevant to the students' and the world's needs. But it cracks doors and opens windows. Also, the fact that society exists in growing crises will make it difficult for universities to revert to promoting value-free academic disciplines. It is more likely that the one exception will become two, and the exceptions will become the norm. Universities will be advertising their contribution to society rather than the rejection of values in their teaching.

Perhaps most remarkable and promising is that the trustees of Columbia University have appointed Nemat "Minouche" Shafik as president of the university. She has written a book entitled *What We Owe Each Other: A New Social Contract.* She is challenging Columbia University to think "how we can better support each other to address inequities and build flourishing societies." This is not for her a matter of a temporary emergency but of how the institutions of a society should normally work. Perhaps academic disciplines at Columbia can reject the goal of being value-free! Perhaps change can spread from there.

What I am criticizing is a form of education that is still deeply entrenched but is probably dying anyway. I am noting that for the past half-century both the curricula and the research of educational institutions have served money, with catastrophic consequences. Of course, it has not even thought about serving God explicitly. But sadly, it has not considered the alternative of serving the creation.

Since education as a whole makes no claim to be Christian and has largely excluded the study of the Bible, we cannot condemn it in terms of its own self-understanding. It has helped a lot of students to get better-paying jobs. It faces a crisis in that half of college graduates now end up in jobs they could have gotten just as well without the college degree. Unless young people find some other reason to go to college, attendance will decline.

University research has contributed to many technological and institutional improvements that increase corporate profits. It has also, and—indeed, thereby—contributed to the drastic worsening of the human prospect. Since university departments do not take advantage of being together in one institution but instead pride themselves on their independence, it is clear that we could train young people to do research in many fields in separate institutions. Getting research done will cease to be a reason to support universities that are also engaged in equipping young people with degrees. For the young people, being certified to do the required research will be a more direct way to a better job.

I have criticized the profound shift of education from the service of society and individual students that was, at least partly, in the service of God, to the predominant and unabashed service of money. But my main point in all of this is that the liberal churches have paid no attention. The culture's shift to atheism is killing the churches, but the liberal church makes no effort to challenge its assumptions and basic commitments. Even in the church, the authority of the university is more respected than that of Jesus.

In short, in this as in so many ways, the service of money destroys those who follow it. The educational institutions began,

at least partly, in the service of God. What they did for young
people in the service of God in fact prepared them for middle class
life and thus benefited them economically. Among the side effects
of institutions organized for the benefit of students and society
was research of various kinds, which benefited both students and
schools.

When these institutions redefined themselves as serving only
money, it turns out that they are inefficient in this respect. Different
kinds of institutions could help students get better-paying jobs more
efficiently. Other kinds of institutions can also do research more
efficiently. A society that serves money will choose the cheapest
way of preparing students to earn money and preparing some to
do specialized research.

To illustrate how the service of money plays out, I could have
described the world of business or the world of politics. They need
desperately to be changed, and we can rejoice that wonderful experiments are going on. They can be changed, and I will return to
that topic when I discuss ecological civilization.

I have focused on education to point out that the service of
money has spread from its strongholds to an area that until recently
it did not control. I have done so because education is an area whose
history has usually been to promote values other than money and to
encourage students to adopt them. For the churches to ignore the
change has been suicidal. It has allowed skepticism with regard to
Christian teaching to dominate society and shape the young people
who are the products of this education into sometimes militant
atheists and anti-Christians. It has seeped into the liberal church
and disabled it from making any serious response.

I would not say that we have ever had a culture and education
that truly and fully served God. But in the past, Western culture
has at least been influenced by the idea that we should serve God.
We can now see the consequences of accepting theoretically, as
well as practically and existentially, the idea that we should look

out for ourselves and make wealth our goal. We Christians have a chance to serve God by noting what is happening and proposing alternatives.

In the previous chapter, I argued that experience and reason support belief in Jesus' Abba. In this chapter, I have suggested that tossing God aside and putting no check on the service of money has led us to the brink of global death. It is time for Christians to live, think, and act as believers in Jesus' Abba. And the first step might be to teach our children that serving only money will destroy both them and a habitable planet.

4

Truth

I AM NOT trying to give an exhaustive picture of Jesus, of Jesus' Abba, or of what it means to be a disciple. I want you to know that when we free Jesus' belief in Abba from later additions and corruptions, we can find support for it in common experience, inescapable assumptions, and facts that have been scientifically established. I also think that attitudes and practices, apart from which the Earth is being destroyed, are strongly supported by belief in Jesus' Abba and discipleship to Jesus. In the process of showing that, I have criticized the dominant scientific community and the way science is taught.

I have implied that scientists put their commitment to atheism above their commitment to evidence. I have denied that they speak with authority on this topic. I am going to describe other topics on which they sometimes claim authority, but in fact are misleading.

The situation has grown worse since World War II. I consider that the organization of the sciences in modern universities is largely responsible.

For centuries, science could speak with great authority on many topics. This is still true on most of them. I check expectations about weather that have been scientifically developed. They are very rarely seriously misleading. Technological feats depend on extreme scientific accuracy and are often wonderfully successful. I will be referring below to what we are learning from pictures taken by the amazing telescope that has recently been put into space.

Hardly less marvelous than the telescope itself was the process of putting it into the right location in space. Everything took place without a hitch. When scientists tell us how to accomplish such feats, they speak with uncontestable authority. What scientists have learned about electronics has created a whole new world that has transformed our lives. To suggest that scientists no longer have authority when they speak about a vast array of topics would be foolish. But, too often, they use their legitimate authority in ways that are misleading and destructive.

But what does this have to do with the teachings of Jesus? He stood in the Hebrew prophetic tradition which, already for eight centuries, had been defined by its readiness to speak truth to power. Modern science developed in a context where a quite nonprophetic Christian church held power, and it takes pleasure in pointing out how courageously its early leaders spoke truth to power. For the prophets of Israel, the great value, alongside truth, was justice. For modern science, it was knowledge. Of course, many Hebrews, Jews, Christians, and Muslims have not prioritized truth. And many scientists, especially in recent decades have emphasized pragmatic concern for their discipline at the expense of depreciating the quest for inclusive truth.

Jesus prioritized speaking truth to power. To be a disciple of Jesus is to try to do so and often to call attention to the failures of the community to prize truth. In one sense, this entire document is a call to truth. This chapter deals especially with the decreasing interest in truth on the part of the modern communities most often looked to for truth.

The most famous advocate for "truth" is Socrates. He noted that in Athens there were many people ready to teach ambitious young men how to persuade others and win arguments. But he did not find anyone who was teaching the truth for its own sake or how to arrive at it. He called for people to seek truth for its own sake. The idea caught on in Athens, giving us the enormous and truly astonishing achievements of Plato and Aristotle. Since then, we have assumed that real scholars care about truth, and that some, especially philosophers and scientists, are dedicated to truth.

A glance at a concordance will assure anyone that Israel highly valued "truth." According to John, Jesus also taught that we should seek the truth, that the truth would set us free. The contexts in Greece and Israel were very different from each other, but they overlapped. Socrates wanted politicians to speak the truth whether or not it helped them persuade others to follow them. In Israel also it meant telling it honestly rather than pleasing the powerful. This is also part of its meaning today.

However, our situation has its special emphases. We are the inheritors of a long conflict between the dominant religious community and the philosophical and scientific communities about what is true. The Christian church had worked out complex creeds to summarize what it taught, and it had developed a system of deciding when it must oppose ideas that were, by that standard, false. Some original seekers of truth were burned at the stake by the church because it was decided that their teaching could not be reconciled with the established "truth."

To this day there are Christians who refuse to accept well-established scientific theories because they conflict with the Bible or authoritative doctrine. The story of this conflict is usually told in these terms. The church defends old teachings despite the fact that their error has been demonstrated. But factual accuracy is not the only, or even the most important, form of truth. Fiction also can convey truth. The church's story conveys truth. Of course, this kind of truth does not preclude the possibility of other true stories. Sometimes the worldview defended by the church has been superior to the one on which the scientific community insists. Sometimes it is the scientific community that clings to its traditions even when some of their ideas have been refuted.

Consider the commitment of modern scientists, from the middle of the seventeenth century to the middle of the nineteenth, to a radical dualism of the human and the natural, both being created out of nothing. The biblical account is of humans as the capstone of the divine creation of nature out of chaos. The scientific dualism led to the idea that nature is matter in motion with no value in itself. The Bible is emphatic that God sees that all creation is good. The whole, including humanity, is very good.

Given this difference, in my view, the church's mistake was to accord far too much authority to science and its accompanying philosophy. One might say that this is old stuff, not relevant to the question of truth now. Yes. But the situation has not improved.

When science accepted evolution and persuaded itself to give up dualism, It clung to its view that nature is mechanical, material, deterministic, and purposeless. This nature now includes human beings. The Bible and Christian teaching generally hold to a more realistic view of human beings and are more open to seeing nature as a whole in organic terms. Too often, excessive deference to science has led Christians to accept some kind of dualism. For example, theologians gave the worldview over to science and turned to existentialism as providing a context to discuss questions about the meaning of life—questions that were excluded by science's stubborn adherence to materialist and mechanistic models.

One could, of course, say that this adherence is not part of science, that science as such is simply seeking truth. We could also say that a church that is not open to learning new truths from philosophy and science is not Christian. I would, indeed, make both statements. But then we are not talking any longer about what is done in the name of science by people who call themselves scientists or in the name of Christianity by people who call themselves Christians. These actual communities have made, and are both making, serious mistakes. Neither, in my view, is giving high priority to truth.

In the chapter on evidence for Jesus' Abba, I dealt at some length with the fact, reluctantly accepted by scientists, that the world is fine-tuned for life. I showed that the simplest explanation is that there is a cosmic purpose at work favoring life. This fits well with Jesus' Abba.

However, the scientific community as a whole is committed to explaining this fine-tuning as a matter of chance. If there have been enough "universes" then the occurrence of fine-tuning in this one need not entail purpose. I have pointed out that this alternative has not even been coherently described. Nevertheless, it is not too much to say that the idea that our universe is one of many is now often presented as part of the scientific worldview. Some Christians, because of their excessive eagerness never to conflict with science, are replacing "universe" with "multiverse."

My view is that a theory for which there is, and can probably never be, any evidence whatsoever, is not a scientific theory. The fact that many scientists accept it does not give it any authority. The idea was invented for no reason except to maintain atheism. Should disciples of Jesus base their thinking on an a priori commitment to atheism? Surely not.

If scientists and philosophers give genuinely scientific and philosophic reasons for disbelief in God, disciples of Jesus should listen carefully, open to persuasion. There have been many ideas of God that do not survive open discussion. But similarly, if scientists and philosophers discover evidence that an aim at more valuable experience has played a role in evolution, they should be open to affirming it.

I have just learned of an incident that expresses the dogmatic opposition to considering God. Herman Daly was a co-founder of the journal of Ecological Economics. Recently he offered it an article evaluating the adequacy of the mechanistic theory of evolution. He thinks it has not explained the rise of the animate from the inanimate or the distinctively human from the generally animal. The reviewer strongly opposed publication.

He does not find any factual errors. But he sees that Daly leaves open the possibility of alternatives to neo-Darwinism. For this crime, he accuses Daly of religious fundamentalism. If the journal publishes anything of this sort, it will damage all who support ecological economics and justify the accusation that it is not scientific.

There is, in fact, a great deal of evidence that human purposes play a role in the world. I think we should follow that evidence even if many scientists choose not to. If the evidence is that an aim at bringing life into being has been at work long before there were any human beings, I favor the theory that includes purpose in the universe.

Scientists have long been forcing all evidence into the requirements of a particular metaphysics. They have discouraged certain lines of inquiry. They have excommunicated those who would not follow the orthodox line. None of this excuses Christians from their crimes against scientists. But the heroic virtues of a few scientists in the past, in serving truth rather than accepting incorrect traditional Christian teaching, do not support treating contemporary scientific heretics in similar ways.

One might say that the only problem is that scientists have been told to accept one set of metaphysical views. And I agree that if scientists would place loyalty to evidence ahead of commitment to seventeenth century metaphysics, disciples of Jesus and scientists committed to truth could work together much better for the salvation of the world.

Nevertheless, we need to recognize that the tendencies to premature closure and excessive authoritarianism are present even when the metaphysics is not involved. I am writing shortly after pictures from the new telescope have become available for study. I am warned that the conclusions I draw have not stood the test of time, that it is premature to build theories on the basis of what we are now able to see. But I can say that the obvious evidence does not support the Big bang theory.

If the idea of the expansion of the universe had been treated from the beginning in a responsible scientific way, as one theory explanatory of the empirically known redshift, this lack of confirmation would be hailed as important help. But from a very early stage, the dominant scientific community has been presenting the Big Bang as part of our scientific knowledge of the universe. Most people in the Christian community have accepted it as scientific fact.

I was told, from a very early stage, that there are other possibilities that the scientific community is ignoring or ridiculing. The one to which I was introduced is ridiculed as the "tired light" theory. Adherents pointed out that, if light slows down a little over ages of time, the red shift can be explained without positing the expansion of the universe. The new pictures of the ancient universe fit this theory better. We are seeing what the universe was like at a time much closer to the time posited for its origins. We would expect to find nothing that appeared to be older than the date given for the Big Bang. Presumably it would be a lot smaller than it is now. So far as I have understood, none of this fits what we see.

Long before these photographs were made, the Big bang theory required the ad hoc positing of a vast amount of dark matter and dark energy. The word "dark" means simply that we have no evidence for it. Having to introduce empirically undiscoverable entities in support of a hypothesis counts against it. In my view before taking this huge step, science should have called the community together to consider other hypotheses. Of course, some of them were "considered." But the tendency was to dismiss them for limitations less serious than the need to posit non-experienceable entities.

It is my impression that one problem is that the authority of Einstein counts against the recognition that light may be affected by the plasma that is dispersed throughout space. Einstein thought the space between the stars was a vacuum, and he proclaimed that in a vacuum the speed of light is constant against it. It is now recognized that there is no vacuum, but scientists are reluctant to consider that plasma might affect the light that passes through it. No one doubted that light was slowed when it passed through water or glass, but there was a strong tendency to keep the speed of light unaffected by plasma. Science calls for treating this assumption as one to be empirically tested.

The new photographs give no support to the big bang theory. The general impression is that the universe at the time we now see it was much like the present one. However, the established leadership plans to consider all sorts of possibilities that could explain this fact other than that the theory is mistaken. It seems unlikely to give much attention to alternative theories. In my view, this commitment to a troubled theory that blocks equal attention to alternatives is not scientific. It simply shows that scientists, even in regard to their scientific work, are much like the rest of us.

Now let us suppose that scientists should decide to act on scientific principles. That would make it easier for Christians to fully support and trust them. But one more change would be needed for them to become ideal partners in the quest to save the world. Scientists would need to recognize that their methods do not apply to all questions about reality. This is not unimaginable.

Some are already saying that they can explain everything except "consciousness."

But some of these scientists think consciousness plays no role in the world. That machines would not be conscious does not mean that they cannot replace human beings. The mechanistic view of nature was part of modern science from the beginning and is thus successfully expanding into the human and mental realms. The astounding and world-transforming explanations offered by science have tended to set the norm for thought of all kinds. The mechanistic explanations of human behavior are pushing aside the humanities, which have generally assumed that humans are responsible beings who are free and unpredictable. The "humanities" have been increasingly marginalized in the university. Social studies aim to be social sciences.

Scientists thus tend to the idea that eventually everything that matters can be explained by science, that is, by necessary and repeatable events. But very few really internalize the implications. Hardly any think of themselves as zombies or robots. It is hard to believe that when I type words into a computer, my conscious thought plays no role at all.

Despite the enormous amount of information about an ant that fits the mechanical model, I still think it is quite different from a grain of sand. If the grain of sand moves, we think something moved it. But most of the movement of the ant seems to be self-initiated. Is there really no fundamental difference between the animate and the inanimate? The question arises whether the simplest elements which have evolved into rocks and mushrooms, trees and beetles, and whales and humans are essentially rocklike, as modern science tends to imply.

We Whiteheadians prefer not to classify events as repeatable or nonrepeatable. Our view is that every event is unique and that there are repeatable elements in all. If scientists accepted as scientists what they assume in daily life, we could have a partnership that could make real progress in shaping the future. History, the story of unique and unrepeatable happenings, could return to the university. We could think together about what is happening and what we should do.

5

The Least of These

ONE OF Jesus' best-known sayings is that what we do to the lowliest of human beings, we do to God (Matthew 25:40). It is a profound teaching, quite central to Jesus' message and, like other teachings of Jesus, quite important for human survival. As with everything in the preceding chapters, it is radically countercultural.

In all human civilizations, there are great differences between the rich, the famous, and the powerful, on the one side, and the poor, the unknown, and the powerless, on the other. Inevitably we have more feelings for the billionaires and the queens, about whom we read in the newspaper, than for the nameless and homeless about whom, as individuals, we are likely to be entirely uninformed. The former are real people, like us, only better known. Whether the "least" of these live or die, we do not know. How can we care?

But for Jesus, just because our society forms us and locates us hierarchically, just because we can often live our lives with no meaningful contact with "the least," it is important to remind ourselves that, before God, we might even say that the least of these are of special concern. God knows and loves everyone. But perhaps those who are most neglected and disregarded in our societies evoke a special tenderness on the part of God.

It would be too much to say that the church has been deeply affected by this teaching. But it has been heard. Christians do know that earthly distinctions of greatness do not translate to anything special for God. Charity, in the sense of giving to the poor, is a widely practiced virtue.

Of course, the implication that we should order society in a more egalitarian way does not have much serious support. Rhetorically, we may approve of the ideal. But, practically, it is far down the list of priorities. Middle class Christians are not really interested in sharing their wealth and comfort with the least of these. As long as it costs us nothing, we wish them well. We may even give to a charity that provides them with food.

The most important thinker in modern times who really cared about the least of these was Karl Marx. There are many questions about his ideas. In at least some instances, following his ideas has led to terrible cruelty. China is ruled by its Communist Party. Although China's current economic policies, in technical matters, are not much influenced by Marx, it is important to note that China has brought eight hundred million people out of poverty as defined by the United Nations. This has been accomplished in a time when, in the rest of the world—where other billions of poor are to be found—poverty has not been reduced.

China's success indicates that excuses should not be accepted. Poverty reduction is an aspect of the changes we need that can be accomplished. The problem is that too few are willing to follow Jesus in putting the poor in first place. Atheist China is putting God's beloved "least" ahead of money. It can be done.

Thus far, despite the vast differences between Jesus' day and ours, I have tried to stay close to statements for which Jesus' support is clear. At this point I am making a jump. I believe that to be a disciple of Jesus today is to give major attention to some matters that were marginal for Jesus.

In the late 1960s, our world was awakened to the decline of its natural ecologies. Many species were disappearing. The ability of the planet to support human life was declining, but the human demand on the natural environment was still growing. The situation was not sustainable. The alternative to change would be catastrophe. This was not the kind of catastrophe from which Jesus hoped to save Israel. But I believe that he calls us, today, to give it priority in our thinking and action. To do so does not ask us to reject the thinking about nature in the Bible as a whole, or specifically that of Jesus. Modify, certainly.

The Bible as a whole has been criticized for affirming human "dominion" over the rest of God's creation. Jesus did not make this criticism. So, in a sense, he shares the blame of the Hebrews generally, along with other civilized people, for imposing the human will on the natural world at the expense of natural ecologies and other species of life. In most respects, Jesus shared the worldview of Jews of his time. His was a human mind. He was not God. Disciples should ask: In what respects and to what degree, should we differ from Jesus in order, at a deeper level, to accord with his teaching? Where do we find guidance?

Having made clear that slavish copying of Jesus' ideas is not true discipleship, let us notice also that, with regard to the human/nature relation, the ideas of modernity are far worse than those of the Hebrews generally and of Jesus specifically. Modernity has been predominantly dualistic even after the acceptance of the fact that humanity evolved in the same process that produced other species. Somewhat incoherently, most modern people still suppose, or at least act as if, the only locus of intrinsic value is in human beings. Some make an exception of pets that have become part of a human family. The value of all the rest is its usefulness to human beings. That usefulness is generally measured by money. Aiming at making money out of nature speeds up the destruction of ecosystems and species.

Israel's creation story declares that God finds value in everything that is created. The implication is that destruction of others is always a loss, even nonhuman others. There is an influential story about God's care that the variety of species be preserved. That human beings dominate all the rest is illustrated in building an ark to save them as well as in killing those that humans find threatening. God's giving humans dominion justifies hunting other animals for food. It certainly justifies killing predators to safeguard human children and to preserve domesticated animals like sheep. Whether it justifies recreational hunting is another question. I doubt it.

How did Jesus see these matters? He thought that God cared for birds and plants. But his teaching does not focus on these. From the fact that God cares for even these, Jesus moves to the assurance that a God who cares for plants and other animals surely cares much more for humans even, perhaps especially, for the least of us.

We, on the other hand, need to speak with the opposite emphasis. God cares for all human beings, but not only for us. Divine care extends to sparrows and wildflowers. We need to follow in caring about the least of these creatures.

This does not contradict Jesus' views, but the emphasis differs markedly. Jesus takes for granted that, as we are taught in Genesis, God cares for all the creatures. He takes for granted that such caring is quite natural. He is not confronting a huge system that denies that nonhuman creatures have any claim on us. To get our society to give any consideration to the wellbeing of other creatures for their own sake, we have to go counter cultural. I think we have Jesus' support, but honesty requires recognition that our focus is different from his.

For example, Jesus is said to have cast evil spirits out of someone and allowed them to enter a herd of swine who then drowned themselves. No doubt he was emphasizing that the healing of one person is worth costing a lot of sacrifice of wealth. But I do not sense that the perspective of the pigs is considered by Jesus any more than it is today in a pork factory. We disciples believe ourselves called to a very different emphasis.

The consequences that have followed this devaluation of all except the human are far more threatening now than they would have been then. Even for the sake of human beings, even if nothing else mattered, close attention to the condition of the nonhuman parts of our environment is now extremely important.

One might argue that all that is necessary is for people to act rationally. In one sense, this is true. To truly act rationally would involve taking even the least of these and the distant future into account. But that kind of rationality will occur only if we have a worldview that strongly pulls us to wider and wider horizons of consideration. Belief in Jesus' Abba can do that. But for most people today, to introduce God in any sense is irrational. The rationality that has taken the place of truly inclusive rationality is taught most clearly in our departments of economics.

I will give an example of how that works out in our economistic world. A Japanese whaling company kills just one species of whale. It is doing so far faster that the whales can reproduce. Someone asked whether it would not be better (more rational) to kill fewer so that the business could be operated longer.

The response was No, they had done their homework. The current rate of killing was the most profitable. When they have wiped out this species, they will have built up substantial capital that can be invested in some other profitable business. To be rational is to make as much money as possible.

We may wonder whether something similar is occurring with our pollinators. About a third of our food depends on them as well as much of the beauty of our gardens. But already forty per cent of our pollinators are faced with extinction. Have our lords and masters calculated that it will be more profitable to destroy our pollinators rather than give up the use of insecticides? Let the human diet be drastically reduced rather than reduce the corporate bottom line!

As explained in earlier chapters, modernity has chosen money as its ultimate value. Because that has happened, the unnecessary extinction of a species of whales is considered rational. And the same logic may support the extinction of our pollinators. The most important need is not "rationality" but a well-chosen end. For the ancient Hebrews, unlike for moderns, the nonhuman world is the kind of thing for which humans can care. To stop destroying it makes sense. To motivate us to do this will require us to care much more intensely about our fellow creatures than Jesus did. It will also require a frontal attack on modern thinking.

Today informing ourselves about what is happening as a result of our lack of care usually is part of the process of change. But cognitive learning, by itself, rarely changes our behavior sufficiently. We usually pigeonhole new information in ways that prevent it from affecting our actions. Or we acknowledge that we should change but admit that it is too hard. We have other priorities.

As we reflect about ourselves, a good topic is food. Jesus did not reflect much about what we eat, but we have said enough now about our different situations. We know, for example, that cows create a great deal of methane gas that contributes significantly to climate change. Raising cows in order to feed us beef is a large industry. Should we continue to support it?

Given my formulation, the obvious answer is No. But matters are always more complicated. There are questions about health, enjoyment, community, practicality, costs, animal wellbeing, alternatives, and so on.

This is not the place for going into all the pros and cons. I personally decided No when I learned more about how industrial methods are applied to the creation of meat. I am appalled by the consequence for the animals, for the environment, and for climate change. On the other hand, in the parable of the prodigal son, Jesus approves of the eating of "the fatted calf" to celebrate the son's return. I think that kind of celebration can still get a Yes. A disciple of Jesus does not favor absolutes.

As long as no community decision is made, all should check out alternatives and make their own decisions. These days it is possible to buy products made from vegetables that are almost indistinguishable from meat. Frankly, in my view, the justifications for a meat diet are disappearing.

But my specific point here is not to answer the question for others. It is to notice that a good many people have decided that it would be better, all things considered, to stop eating beef, but then continue to do so. Customs and habits are deep-seated and rarely changed by a simple decision. We are more likely to change if we visit a meat factory and watch the slaughtering of animals than if we simply read about it. Sometimes indirectly related experiences change behavior. The actual experience of miserable heat will lead some people to ask how they can contribute to slowing global warming. Since we all eat, and most people eat meat, this is one of many topics that deserve a consideration we do not find in Jesus.

Decisions about different kinds of meat may differ. A still greater difference exists between meat and fish. In Jesus' Galilee, fish were extremely important to the diet. There is no hint that Jesus doubted its appropriateness. My original decision was in favor of continuing to eat seafood. I am less and less sure that is the right decision for me, now, in Southern California, but I have not changed my behavior. I need to do more serious study of what goes on in the production of fish for my table.

Although our questions are different from those in Jesus' day, a glance at Genesis shows that the question of justifying the killing and eating of other animals is not new. It is striking that in the passage in which humans are told to have dominion over all the other animals, both other animals and humans are still expected to eat only plants. It is only after the flood that humans are specifically authorized to eat other animals.

Today the question arises again. Some people are developing a real sense of being part of the animal world, of treating other animals with respect, of calling them individually by name. For them, the idea of killing and eating these fellow creatures is abhorrent. Some believe that until we care for individual members of other species and feel for them as Jesus taught us to feel for "the least of these," we will fall short of the love that God models, the love of all living things.

There are other implications of our new emphasis on nonhuman nature. We listen appreciatively to the remnants of indigenous people who have preserved practices long considered stupid by self-confident moderns. Obviously, we cannot go back. Individuals, nevertheless, can experiment with living more naturally. If, as some of us expect, the coming chaos will end many practices that depend on large-scale organization, some things which we have thought of as irretrievable may turn out to be the only possibility.

Think about a baby's milk. In modernity we assumed that it was better for baby's milk to come from cows, through commercial processes of production, packaging, transportation, and sale. That mothers might nurse their own babies seemed completely out of date. This way fathers can participate equally in feeding babies. Mothers are liberated for "civilized" activities. Some mothers, now, are wondering whether, humanly and naturally, something is lost.

Overall, the separation of babies from their parents in lying-in hospitals expresses the de-naturalizing of relationships within the family. It is expressed also with regard to sexuality. Sexuality has always been important, also in other animals. But the obsession with sexuality is a product of the modern invention of adolescence.

Just in the period when sexual feelings have greatest urgency, youth are denied opportunity to express them healthily. In most of the world and in pre-modern times, children married in their early teens. Their sexuality was channeled in a context which might produce babies. It strengthened the mutual commitment of marriage. Sexual repression and irresponsible sexual behavior were far less evident in society. Today, we marvel why a teacher like Jesus has so little to say about a problem that obsesses us. The answer is that the adolescence that creates the problem did not exist. Children paired off young.

The scientists who warned us that our modern practices were destroying the capacity of nature to support us were ecologists. They study the complex systems of mutual dependence that have developed in nature. They show us that when some species become scarce or even extinct, this triggers the collapse of the whole system. This possibility intensifies the importance of some of the least of these.

On the other hand, it shows the importance of scientific knowledge. The disappearance of many other species has little effect on the wellbeing of the ecological system. The system can easily adjust. The loss of species may still be felt as an impoverishment of the whole, but in comparison with the collapse of whole systems, the loss is minor.

We need the guidance of scientists to supplement our feelings of care for the least of these. For example, it is more important that we care for the insects that pollinate than for most others. It is astonishing to me that we have killed so many of these and based our agriculture on practices that still reduce these populations.

To care for the soil may seem sentimental, but soil is full of living creatures. These have in the past absorbed much of the surplus carbon from the atmosphere. Our commercial agriculture is based on poisoning pests in ways that also poison the organisms that turn inanimate dirt into living soil.

If we restored our soil to health, we could go a long way toward ending the climate change that is threatening the habitability of the planet. Sadly, this possibility is barely mentioned, because it would require major changes in our system of producing food.

I conclude with a confession. I do not love all of the "least of these" when we extend Jesus' teaching to our fellow creatures. In particular, I do not love mosquitoes. I hope they are not an important part of any ecological system. My feelings go back to the teaching of domination. I want to dominate the mosquitoes and kill them when I can. As a disciple of Jesus, I am glad that the extension of his call for special concern for the "least of these" to all living things was not part of his teaching.

Can we justify making such distinctions? I hope so. Love is especially meaningful when directed to creatures that experience our love and love us in return. It makes a difference for any creature that feels pleasure and pain. It is also meaningful when directed to creatures who are important for the ecosystems. It may not be important if there are creatures whose wellbeing depends on communicating diseases to the higher animals and especially to us. We should love most biotics, but perhaps not all. We should love most insects, but perhaps not all.

We are called to love the Earth. We are called to love the whole life system. We are called work for its healing and health. We must not return to the anthropocentrism of our ancestors, especially our modern ones. But a disciple of Jesus hesitates to turn statements of this kind into absolutes. For the good of the whole, we may need to eliminate some elements, or at least control them, for the sake of others.

6

The Basileia Theou Today— Ecological Civilization

ALL OF JESUS' teaching was under the general heading of the "basileia theou." That this was his overarching commitment is clear from the fact that the heart of the prayer he taught his disciples was that God's basileia come. Both Matthew and Mark state that his message, as he began his ministry, was that the basileia theou was "at hand." Matthew tells us that this had also been the message of John, into whose movement Jesus was baptized (Matthew 3:2).

If we want to be disciples of Jesus, we need to think more about Jesus' inclusive message. What is the "basileia theou"? What does it mean to say that it is "at hand"?

The Lord's Prayer tells us that the basileia theou is equivalent to God's will being done. In previous chapters, we have seen that would mean loving everyone, and, in particular, loving enemies. It would mean knowing and experiencing God as an intimate parent rather than a mighty king. It would mean serving God rather than money. It would mean seeking truth and speaking it even when that is costly. And, given the danger today of the collapse of essential natural ecologies, it would mean keen attention to, and concerned care for, our fellow creatures. Of course, Jesus has much more to say about his Abba and being his disciple, and we look to his life to see the basileia in action.

How best to translate "basileia theou"? The church has chosen to translate basileia as "kingdom." It is true that over the centuries most basileia have been kingdoms. But the term basileia says nothing about how it is ruled. It is simply a politically defined region, a country. A basileia could be a republic. Many modern Christians think that Jesus' teachings generally favor that form of government.

In the form in which the church has taught the prayer, a sentence has been added to what Jesus taught. We conclude the prayer by telling God that the reason we pray to him is that his is the power and glory and, again, kingdom. This tells us a lot about the church, but it does not fit well with Jesus' Abba. Since the term basileia is open-ended with respect to how it is ruled, and since Jesus depicts God as one who tenderly cares for all, I suggest that the connotations of "commonwealth" are closer to Jesus' understanding of a world in which God's will is done.

I propose a change also at the beginning of the Lord's prayer. We pray to our Father who is in heaven. What did Jesus or the early church mean by locating God "in heaven"? Did they think that if we went far enough "up" we would reach the place where God lives? Perhaps some thought that way. But the idea that God is far away is certainly in tension with Jesus' teaching about his Abba. I doubt that Jesus thought of heaven as a limited location within the whole. I think his meaning would be captured better by speaking of our heavenly Father in distinction from our earthly father.

One support for this kind of shift is that in the gospels we find that the language is sometimes "the Kingdom of Heaven." This is hard to understand as a location at a distance from the Earth. The term "heavenly commonwealth" would work better.

Thus far I am proposing changes that I consider justified by reflection on what Jesus was thinking. But while I'm at it, I want to make another change on the grounds that it would help us two millennia later. There is still a section of our population for whom speaking of a heavenly commonwealth makes sense. But for many people the idea of "heaven" or "heavenly" is meaningless or silly. There is probably no solution to this problem, but the adjective "divine" seems to me clearer. For me, what in most Bibles is translated either Kingdom of God or Kingdom of Heaven is better named "the divine commonwealth."

Now, we can ask, what does it mean that a world in which God's will is done, a divine commonwealth, is "at hand"? This is the language of the King James translation. Some recent translations say is "coming." I believe that, in this instance, the King James translation is better.

"Is coming" sounds like a prediction. If Jesus predicted that God's will was going to be done on Earth soon, he was simply mistaken. In any case, although such a prediction might have been encouraging, it did not make demands on its hearers. To say that something is "at hand" means that it is available and accessible. The question is whether we will grasp it when the act of grasping may require sacrifice and lead to suffering.

There was a possibility of transforming the relation to Rome in such a way that it was no longer repressive or oppressive. That would require loving the Romans. That was not impossible. It was "at hand." It could be chosen. And certainly, the Romans would not have destroyed Jerusalem and expelled all Jews from their holy land if the Jews had adopted this stance toward Romans.

More broadly, the kind of life that would be faithful to God could be chosen in personal relationships. Some people did make that choice, and Jesus saw that as participation in the divine commonwealth. For two thousand years people have read Jesus' teachings about the divine commonwealth as showing how to live rightly in any context. Jesus would not object.

Jesus was not announcing that this was going to happen. Even on the simplest personal matters, he did not know whether his hearers would change their habits and practices. They could. The new life was possible. It was "at hand." Jesus hoped that people would change, and he did what he could to encourage people to take what was at hand, whatever the cost, so as to save Israel.

Some might say that the failure of the Jews to follow Jesus' way means that all of this is now irrelevant. The choice between saving Israel from oppression and a self-destructive response is now irrelevant. But the choice between saving the world and following the course we are now on is far from irrelevant. I know no other way to follow Jesus closely today than to make it known that a healing alternative is "at hand."

Jesus did not predict success in his day. Indeed, Mark (13:2) tells us that when Jesus was in Jerusalem, he predicted the destruction of the temple. By that time, at least, he foresaw that he had failed to redirect Israel away from suicidal revolts. Realistic prediction was not alien to Jesus. Perhaps by then he did not think that the alternative was at hand. The Jewish leadership was working with Rome to eliminate him.

We can predict that a great deal of suffering is now inevitable. Our task, however, is to emphasize what is still possible, still at hand. We cannot predict that what is at hand will be chosen. Jesus proclaimed the possibility, indeed the fact, that the divine commonwealth was at hand, as good news. If we can honestly say that avoiding the worst horrors that we are bringing upon ourselves is possible, indeed, readily possible, that it is at hand, we can be bearers of urgently needed good news today.

Much of this manuscript is spelling out my recommendation for understanding what the divine commonwealth would be. It would prevent the worst horrors toward which we are now heading from occurring. In this chapter, I want to show how natural and proper it is for us who claim to follow Jesus to describe what today corresponds with what he called the divine commonwealth.

What was the fate from which Jesus hoped to save Israel? It was the destruction of Israel. He proposed a way of saving Israel that was really possible, although it would require radical change. What is the fate from which we hope to save the Earth? It is the destruction of the natural order, which has been so favorable to human life, and the collapse of social order. Those of us who today are committed to the divine commonwealth propose ways to transform the social order and to save the habitable environment—ways that are really possible but require radical change.

The divine commonwealth is about living in peace with others, willing the good even of enemies. It is supporting life in all its forms, and especially human life, even when that is costly to us. It is being committed to truth, even above the success of particular projects, and to speaking truth to power, even at personal risk. A divine commonwealth would not oppose all competition, but it would keep the competition in the context of a more fundamental cooperation.

Jesus named the transformed world for which he called the "divine commonwealth." We name it "ecological civilization." Jesus addressed the Jewish people about the salvation of Israel. He used language that made sense to them. We Christians may want to keep that language. We may continue to call Jesus our Messiah, or Christ, and call what we hope for the divine commonwealth.

But because that language does not make clear that the whole of the natural world is involved, some of us prefer "ecological civilization." And because salvation is not possible if only Christians are involved in the needed transformation, we need to use secular terms. So, "ecological civilization" is better terminology most of the time.

Drawing the analogy closely may not lead to optimism. Even though Jesus was correct that the divine commonwealth was at hand, and one could get a glimpse of it here and there, most Jews did not reach out to it. The Jewish leadership cooperated with Rome in crucifying him. Relations with Rome remained oppressive and repressive. Jews continued to hate Romans and repeated a hopeless armed struggle. The Romans had finally had enough. They scattered the Jews through the empire and destroyed Jerusalem.

Jesus failed. What are our chances?

If we had taken what was "at hand" two or three decades ago, we might have saved a lot. Since then, thousands of species of life have been eradicated. What is at hand now does not include them. Nor does it include a return to the widely favorable weather we enjoyed then. It does not include all the coral reefs we had then. Probably the melting of glaciers cannot be stopped; so, the oceans will rise and flood half of Bangladesh and some now densely populated land such as Manhattan. Almost certainly some atolls will be uninhabitable. On and on. And then, when the Tibetan glaciers are gone, the Indus and Ganges, the Yangtze and the Yellow River will all run dry. The livelihoods of a billion people will be gone. But that does not mean that nothing worthwhile can be saved, that there is no good news about what is still at hand.

Our global leaders are making commitments to use less of the fossil fuels that contribute to global warming. They are limited in three ways. First, none of them want to take steps that will be highly unpopular with their people. Second, many are beholden to corporations that remain more concerned about their short-term profits than about the long-term wellbeing of life. Third, the great powers keep spending more on their military in complete disregard of the consequences, because their policies conflict with one another and they think they must prepare for war.

Ecological civilization is at hand. But it requires subordinating all these considerations to that one possibility of healthy survival. Thus far nations are not even discussing this alternative.

There is virtually no possibility of avoiding extreme catastrophe without the cooperation of the two great superpowers, the United States and China. At least since September 11, 2001, the United States has sought to be the one dominant power in the world. It has rightly seen that China increasingly competed successfully. The alternative to sharing power was to force China to adopt a subordinate role. This could be done relatively easily on the basis of an enormous superiority in nuclear weapons, but China was about to catch up even in that way. If the United States was to be the sole great power in the world, it had to act quickly while its great nuclear superiority was not challenged. It did so.

The military focus on Russia has intensified. NATO is throwing its power behind Ukraine and crossing lines that it knows may precipitate Russian use of nuclear weapons. Russia may follow China in yielding to NATO's overall military superiority, and the United States may move forward toward its goal of global domination.

But European commitment to Russia's destruction may weaken as the price paid by the people of Europe and the threat of nuclear war rise. The U.S. may have to soften its opposition to negotiation; Russia may emerge as strong as ever; and the alliance of Russia and China will become an alternate global center to the United States and Europe. Or there may be a nuclear war. Germany and the United States seem to have agreed to risk it. We live in profoundly uncertain times.

What must be reversed includes the dominant trend of the economy. The transnational corporations have created a global economy in which everyone depends on goods produced at a great distance. Concentrating production is accompanied by reduced competition among the corporations and increases their ability to control markets. All these factors concentrate wealth and power in fewer and fewer hands.

These corporations, that largely control the government of the United States, seek a world in which the decisions that matter to them are made in a single country, the United States. This requires that Russia and China lose their capacity to make their own decisions in major matters. Their resistance means war.

Even when there is no fighting, the unipolar world sought by the transnational corporations is not sustainable. It produces a gap between the few billionaires and the masses of the poor that is inherently unsettling. For an increasing number of people, the struggle to survive may be desperate. If so, we can see that, objectively, their actions make matters worse, desperate people do not give priority to protecting the existing social order.

Their actions speed up its inevitable collapse. This collapse includes the breakdown in many places of the systems of garbage collection, water, and electricity. Transportation systems become unreliable. Food produced at a distance, on which people have become dependent, cannot be procured. Social chaos harms the movement of essential goods. Local communities will be thrown back on their own resources. Billions of people will die.

The concentration of wealth is also the concentration of power. In many places, governments already serve the rich and their corporations more than they serve their people. The United States is one of those places. Nevertheless, it must find a way to organize the world economically and politically that reverses the centralization of production, control, and wealth. A world organized from the bottom up has a much better chance of becoming an ecological civilization.

The possibility at hand is for local communities to organize themselves so that they can survive even when transportation systems collapse. In food, water, healthcare, and energy, they need to be self-sufficient. Communities may move in this direction only in response to growing chaos, but this will also provide the nucleus for building an ecological civilization. The less they depend on goods and services from others, the less control will the great corporations have over them. In most cases, they will be able to choose their own leaders with little influence of wealth.

Most local communities will want to preserve and improve the land, water, and air. Also, they will care about the trees and the birds. People there will want their children to enjoy the environments they have enjoyed. When people are empowered to choose, far more will choose sustainable practices and policies than great wealth for the few. Communities that are self-sufficient will not have to be obedient to transnational corporations.

"Local communities" remains ambiguous. I think of neighborhoods and quite small towns as the first level. At that level communities can be face to face. I would encourage even these quite small communities to aim to feed themselves and handle the education of their children, among other things.

Equally important with freeing local communities from control by transnational corporations is how they relate to one another. Sometimes strong and healthy communities use their strength to weaken and even to control their neighbors. An ecological civilization will be possible only if these local communities relate to each other in a spirit of community. We need communities of communities.

If the local communities of which we have been speaking are urban neighborhoods, they will flourish only if they work together for the wellbeing of the city. Cities, together with the surrounding countryside, need to cooperate with other cities in a healthy nation. The nation would then be a community of communities of communities.

There are many examples of cooperation at these levels. Often nations command the commitment of people more than the smaller regions in which they live. Rethinking nations as communities of communities of communities will be important.

For centuries something like this characterized the nations of Europe in their inner lives. However, relations among nations were mainly competitive. Competition sometimes took the form of war. The devotion to individual nations that created healthy communities among the people of France and among the people of Germany, led to terrible wars between France and Germany. The agreement of France and Germany after World War II to form a European community has shown that nations can be communities of their own internal communities and then, also, members of a community of nations. This possibility lies at hand. In Europe it has been realized.

There needs to be, however, another step. Currently we see Europe as a community of nations fighting against Russia. If Latin America became a community of nations only to fight with Africa, which would be another community of nations, there would certainly be no ecological civilizations. We need a community of communities of national communities.

Of course, some economic issues would be dealt with at the global level. But since local communities would control local economies that met basic needs, and most of what cannot be handled at the lowest level would be handled at the levels up to the national, only a few economic decisions would depend on the community of nations and very few on the global community. There would, of course, be police forces at all levels, but weapons of mass destruction would be destroyed. The huge sums of money that now are spent on so-called defense, could be devoted to meeting human needs and restoring the health of the natural ecologies in which humans will be nested.

Even with a structure of this kind, the global calamities that are already beginning, such as the floods and extreme heat in Northern India and Pakistan, will not be stopped. But it may be possible all around the world to create small communities that make a good life for their children despite chaotic weather. We can stop poisoning the land, and a healthy topsoil can be recreated. The oceans cannot return to their former cleanliness and riches, but improvements are possible. Certainly, they need not grow more polluted. They can probably never support again the fullness of the ecosystems that characterized them until recently, but they can continue to support a lot of life.

We do not know in detail what is still possible, but we do know that much is still at hand that we are collectively still degrading and destroying. Probably European nations whose people have been shocked by this summer's heat will pressure their governments to take environmental matters more seriously. But there is little indication that the government of the United States will declare its independence from the corporations that have pushed it into global imperialism.

Is an awakening possible? It is still possible that a catastrophe of large proportions will awaken and arouse many people to recognize that life is more precious than money. The people of the world may finally choose survival over the increase of wealth by the wealthy. But if the catastrophes occur elsewhere, there is danger that the American people will be kept blind and ignorant. Still, I believe an awakening is at hand.

That awakening is unlikely apart from a crisis far greater than any that has occurred so far. Some of us think that clarifying in advance what directions should be taken might prove helpful when people are finally forced to change. We think a name for what is still at hand, what could still be done if we rethought and reorganized and recommitted, might help. We feel called not only to offer a name but also to think as much as we can about what patterns of organization and action might contribute to its realization.

Thus far I have used "ecological civilization" to mean simply what is best among real possibilities. But thinking about ecological civilization has led to many specific proposals that are integrated with one another. David Korten has provided a beautiful statement of what an ecological civilization would be like. The Institute for Ecological Civilization is but one of those that have developed fairly clear ideas that are already at hand and may be chosen instead of chaos.

Presenting a picture of the ecological civilization that is at hand has not been fruitless. Under many names, important experiments in change are taking place. Jesus saw the divine commonwealth already occurring from time to time. We can see ecological civilization being actualized more and more, here and there.

The term "ecological civilization" points immediately to a reversal of the way civilization has dealt with nature in the past. People will also change in their relations with each other. The key term here is "community." That term is already widely used. A sustainable and enjoyable civilization will be based on communities and on communities of communities.

By a "community," I mean a group of people who take some responsibility for one another. They may compete in many ways, but at a deeper level they support one another for the sake of the group to which they belong. A family is a community. A congregation is a community. A nation is a community. The European community is a community of nations.

Other aspects of ecological civilization are being actualized on a large scale in China. The Chinese are committed to making sure that their economic growth does not further damage their environment, and they are working to heal some of the damage done to it in the past. Provincial governors are evaluated equally on environmental improvement and economic growth. The government saw that much is lost when most people live in huge cities. It is working hard, and with some success, to encourage many to choose rural villages instead of cities. Ecological civilization means a lot more than that, but that does not negate the improvements that have been achieved.

I am more familiar with what has happened in Pomona,

California, in the few years since it joined the Compassionate Cities movement. The mayor embodies a commitment, and instead of continuing a long history of decline, the people look forward to great things for the city. They are already happening. The leaders in policing and schooling have studied "restorative justice," and the results have been good. Devon Hartman has created a nonprofit business and built a factory to produce solar panels. He has a patent for a new kind that is much more efficient. He is employing local people, and the panels will go first, without charge, to the homes of the poor.

Much more is in process. A group is working toward Pomona producing its own food. There is also the beginning of applying the ideas of a "donut economy." A program has begun to get major institutions to spend their money locally so the local businesses can flourish and enrich the city as a whole. A locally owned bank is being considered. The mayor and the city council are enthusiastically supporting all these efforts and more. The school system is attracting helpers who are skilled at working with those who are having problems with their studies. We are hoping that Pomona can become a model of self-transformation that will be widely followed. A city that is populated by proud citizens, produces its own food and energy, and makes decisions about its own finances has a chance to survive the collapse of many of the structures on which we now rely.

Pomona is in Los Angeles County. Los Angeles County has articulated goals that, if fully actualized, would turn it into a model for ecological civilization. Sadly, it has not given much attention to how to get from here to there. We hope that it will be inspired by Pomona. Pando Populus is involving universities in programs designed to bridge the gap between aspiration and attainment. There are hundreds of other positive developments within the county. Maybe, just maybe, it can become a global leader.

I have spoken of progress near my home. I hope that many

people can cite great examples where they live. Although we must work at the global level to stop global warming, we must also work locally to develop communities that can survive climate chaos.

7

Overcoming the
Western Worldview

To leap from the explicit teaching of Jesus, and the drastic challenge he offers to typical beliefs and actions, to something so supposedly abstract as a worldview may seem a serious mistake. But we Christians should understand that how we think about the world plays a large role in how we act. Worldview questions have appeared in previous sections. They were important in the chapter about the evidence for Jesus' Abba, the discussion of what has happened to higher education, and in talking about the natural sciences in the chapter on truth. Indeed, my worldview has played a role in all that I have written, and I have not concealed my interest in overcoming the modern one. Even so, there is more to be said about the modern worldview and how it is giving way to a new one.

The modern worldview has been closely associated with the amazing progress in science and technology. We certainly must admire this. But it has also done great harm. For example, we have thought that the natural world has no value in itself. When we speak of its value, all too often we mean only its use to us and the enjoyment it provides for us. This anthropocentrism expresses itself in economic theory, in business practice, and in our legal systems. Our resultant actions have led us to take suicidal behavior as normal.

It is, of course, possible to seek to change behavior without discussing the beliefs it expresses. We seek to partner with all who will work for needed changes. Those committed to the modern worldview do not want to end human civilization. Retaining the worldview does not in principle prevent making major changes in behavior. For many, the solution to problems is sought chiefly by legal and technological changes. Perhaps the structure of business activity can improve together with changes in tax policy.

It would be foolish indeed to oppose changes of this sort just because they leave the worldview unchanged. However, it is also foolish to suppose that our worldview does not matter, once we have seen how it has in fact worked out. I'm glad to say that increasing numbers of people understand that how we see the world affects how we treat it.

I propose that we think about worldviews in general and how they come to influence us even when they are not articulated. Let's first note that the modern worldview expresses the characteristic prejudice of the West for seeing and what is seen. Western thinkers build much more on this than on hearing and what is heard. Sight is thought to give a more authentic sense of what is real than hearing or any other sense. This is expressed in almost all Western philosophy and science.

We can trace the priority of the visual world in Western philosophy back to the Greeks. But they were not so attentive to the question of the sources of knowledge as thinkers became in the modern period. They affirmed much on the basis of common sense.

The first philosophers who thought we could only decide what to believe when we focused on how we gain information about the world were the British empiricists. They thought that when they examined how we gained information they could judge more reliably which ideas about the world were accurate.

They were convinced that our knowledge of the world arose in experience, and that our knowledge of the world exterior to our bodies came to us through our sense organs. These included eyes and ears but also touch, taste, and smell. They thought that these provided the data for all thinking about the world, such as that done by scientists. Most scientists agreed.

This position was called empiricism. To make clear that they were not allowing supernatural revelation, or dreams, or imagination as part of the experience that could provide a basis for reliable thinking about the world, their position can be called sensory empiricism. The evidence about the world exterior to our bodies is limited to what we learn through our sense organs.

At this point I am not wanting to evaluate this form of empiricism. The point I want to make is that after acknowledging that we learn about the world through multiple sense organs, in fact, they limited their discussion to what we learn through the eyes. They do not announce that they ignore the other senses. They do not provide arguments for doing so. They seem to assume that their readers will not need any explanation.

The most rigorous and influential of these empiricists was David Hume. Perhaps the most influential feature of his thought was his quest to understand efficient causation empirically. This led him to examine his experience very rigorously.

He shows that we typically think we see a causal relationship when we observe a repeated pattern of change from one situation to the next. But what we see is one state of things and then a slightly different state of things. We find that whenever we create the earlier pattern the later one occurs. We believe there is a causal relation between the two. But Hume saw that all we see are regular patterns of succession. We do not see a cause.

Hume reported his empirical findings, and these greatly influenced Immanuel Kant. Between them, they greatly influenced the course of Western philosophy. This influence continues to this day.

Now my point here is that if Hume had investigated other senses, he would have found that we do have experience of causation. Touch and taste are far more important in shaping our conviction that there are causes and effects than sight. If instead of only looking, he had engaged in wrestling and had his shoulder forced down on the mat, he would have felt a cause. True, someone watching could only report a succession of visual experiences. Why did Hume not extend his investigation in these directions?

One might dismiss this as simply his idiosyncrasy. But we note that Kant and hundreds of other philosophers have accepted this move from not seeing to not experiencing. That few if any have felt a need to justify this move says something about our culture. "Seeing is believing." Hearing, touching, feeling, tasting, and smelling are irrelevant to knowledge in modern Western civilization.

Now, if all cultures agreed on the priority of seeing, we might simply assume that this is the result of human experience universally. But this is far from the case. In their quest for knowledge and understanding, the people of ancient Israel gave priority to hearing.

Of course, they did not neglect seeing in the way Western philosophers have neglected hearing. For example, they occasionally spoke of the wonder of "seeing God." But there is far more in the Bible about hearing God. Ordinarily, the experience of God for them is being called. The scriptures are the "Word of God." They did not paint pictures of God. The creation story is also quite striking. God speaks the world into existence.

A world of hearing is an interpersonal world. When we hear speech, we experience it as meanings being proposed to us by another. We can often report the meaning of what is heard without reproducing the sounds. We do not infer the existence of other people from an initial sensory experience of a meaningless sound. The heart of the world of hearing is interpersonal communication experienced as such. That there is another is not inferred from a series of sounds. It is inherent in the hearing of the meaning.

To clarify the contrast, in the visual field, the whole field is present in each moment. Its temporal character is not essential to it. In the auditory world, the units take time in order to be. In the visual field, the patches of color are accompanied by a sense that they inhere in something. There is a sense that their appearance depends on their inherence in something substantial. In the auditory world there is no sense that some substance underlies the meaning of the phrase.

In sum, the language that develops out of visual experience is a subject/predicate language. The box is brown. The language that develops out of auditory experience highlights events. Running up the hill was exhausting. In the former case, nouns and pronouns seem primary. They are felt to be substantial. In the latter case, verbs and gerunds come to the fore. Processes are fundamental.

The Hebrew God is a communicator of meanings. The meanings often call for action. The resultant actions may be just right, but sometimes they are not. They miss the mark. People are responsible for missing the mark. Sin is real and important.

Some biblical authors assumed that it was important that one's good actions outweigh one's sins. Belief in justice led many to fear for themselves, although they might take some satisfaction in the expectation that those who flourished now, by taking advantage of the weak, would ultimately be punished.

Jesus was a leader in an alternative understanding. There is no doubt that many miss the mark and that some come closer to hitting it. Some are more virtuous that others. But God loves all. Evil deeds often have negative consequences for the perpetrator, but these are not divine punishments. God sends rain to the vicious as well as the virtuous. Our responding to God's call is because we love both God and the world which God loves, including sinners. As we realize God's unconditional love for us and all the ways in which we benefit from it, we want to serve God by serving those whom God loves, all people, and perhaps more.

The world of sight leads in a different direction. We do not immediately see meanings. We see patterns of color. We suppose that these colors inhere in something. The colors change, sometimes drastically. A house painted white may be repainted brown. But it is the same house. Thus, we live in a world of entities that are colored, but in and of themselves are open to diverse colors. Our experience of colors quickly leads us to think in terms of entities that are colored but remain the same when the colors change. These things are what make up the natural world.

In this worldview, humans are different. They are the ones who see and interpret what is seen. Nature is purely objective, that is, the object of sight and of human actions. Humans are active and responsible, being entities of this kind. But they also have capacities that other things do not. The most common response is a dualism. Nature is composed of physical entities in relative motion. Humans perceive and think about these things. Humans have value in themselves. Nature has value for human beings. Indeed, much of what the empiricists thought about human beings derived from the Hebrew contribution to Western culture. Nature obeys natural laws. Humans are free and responsible and should obey moral laws.

The world of hearing encourages storytelling and historical thinking. We will return to this in the next chapter. Hearing leads to process thinking, but there are other process traditions as well. By definition they do not think in terms of substances. My central point here is that there is a close connection between the world of sight and the philosophy of substance. Long before the modern era, thinkers of India who wanted to penetrate to the depths of reality understood those depths to be substances. They were particularly interested in the ultimate substance of all things, which they call Brahman, and their own ultimate substance which they called Atman. They aimed to existentially realize, through profound meditation, that the self or Atman is also Brahman.

One Indian thinker, Gautama, saw that there is no evidence for substances. He taught that there is no Atman and no Brahman. What is, is the ongoing flow of phenomena. This was for him a profound liberation. This understanding, when deeply and existentially understood, is "enlightenment." The enlightened one is a Buddha. Buddhism was the first "process" philosophy. Its metaphysics is very similar to that of Alfred North Whitehead: the many become one and are increased by one.

I am not suggesting that Western philosophers are responsible for their predilection for sight. My point is that philosophy is heavily influenced by the culture in which it is formed. The greatest formative feature of a culture is its language. We think in a language. The language encourages us to think in a certain way.

There is a great family of languages that give expression to the world of vision. They are called the Indo-European languages. These languages encourage us to think of the world as composed of enduring substances with changing appearances.

I noted that Gautama Buddha declared that there are no substances. It is noteworthy that he has had few followers in India. The Indian languages are built around subjects to which a variety of attributes or actions can be attributed. It is very difficult to think in a language against the worldview the language assumes. Gautama's ability to do so is truly remarkable, but few Indians understood him or found him convincing.

However, when Gautama's thought reached China, it was quickly and widely appreciated. The Chinese language is not centered around a noun or pronoun subject. The sentence centers on the verb. It is about what happened. That, of course, includes various entities, but it is not about them. This is true also of Korean and Japanese.

The openness of Chinese to ideas that are on the fringe of Indo-European thought has been illustrated again recently. We American process thinkers have to think against our language. It is a substance language deriving from the world of vision. In process thought, we think there are no substances. We are not admitted into normal university philosophical discussion.

When Zhihe Wang introduced our work into China, within a short time, thirty universities created centers to discuss it! For them it is fitting into Western substance thinking that is hard work. What we process thinkers have to say makes immediate sense.

One reason that some of us cling to ideas that our language discourages is that the natural sciences need it. Based on visual experience, scientists assumed that the natural world is ultimately composed of tiny little material particles. There is now undisputed evidence that it is not. The quantum world cannot be understood that way. Thinking of interconnected events is much more promising.

David Bohm was widely recognized as one of the few deep thinkers about the quantum world. He spent a week or two with us at the Center for Process Studies. He did not become a part of the Whiteheadian community. He stuck with the language he had already developed, but he agreed with Whitehead's understanding. He told me that until Western scientists replaced nouns and pronouns with gerunds in their speech, they would not be able to understand the quantum world.

Scientists as a community resist process thinking. For example, in physics the ultimate entities are thought of as mass and energy. Mass is connected in their minds with the philosophical notion of matter. They consider mass as the fundamental notion and define energy in terms of it: $E=mc^2$. Now, the evidence contradicts this. By that formula, if there were no mass there could be no energy.

But in fact, the evidence is that there is lots of energy where there is no mass.

The photons of light are but one example. Clearly energy is the fundamental character of reality that sometimes also has mass. Scientists in general prefer not to notice this. "Energy" suggests something happening. "Mass" can be understood as something static and substantial. The typical language of American scientists is still a long way from avoiding the habits of mind built into the English language. The evidence is overwhelming that energy is more fundamental than mass, that events are more fundamental than static entities, that processes are more fundamental than substances. When scientists finally pay attention to their own discoveries, they will be able to recover a coherent science as an important contribution to an adequate worldview.

Whitehead's model to replace substance is to see the world as made up of events, each of which is a creative development out of the whole past. Human experiences are such events. The empiricists who thought of humans as individual, separate substances thought that they are related to the external world only by sense experience. Whitehead affirms that we are constituted by our relations to the whole past. Our senses do not give us a clear understanding of efficient causes. Whitehead understands these as the way the past flows into the present, forming the present. We feel ourselves efficiently constituted by the past, but we also feel ourselves forming and reforming that growing past moment by moment.

Clearly, a different understanding of what is most fully actual leads to a different understanding of relationships, including, especially, causal relationships. Whitehead offers the scientific community a way to understand what it is studying that will fit with what it does and with what it learns far better than an understanding based on vision alone. A coherent science lies at hand.

Precisely because their current account of the world is so chaotic, most scientists now insist they do not need a worldview, that worldviews don't matter. This does not deter them from forbidding any worldview that includes God. But it excuses their inability to give sensible answers to important questions. They feel that the enormous achievements of modern science sanction any position it wishes to take. But this is not a stable situation. Science will evolve.

I have elsewhere pointed out that the problem is not just that the ideas of most scientists do not match the implications of scientific discoveries. I conclude by reminding us that science is inherently limited in what it can study. It studies best what can be repeated frequently in a laboratory. Of course, it can also learn a great deal about a world that is not so easily controlled but is still constituted of repeatable elements. It cannot deal with radically unique events.

Sadly, its tendency is to say that what cannot be dealt with by science is not important, perhaps cannot exist. Thus, history and moral responsibility are excluded from having a role to play in the world. In my view, they remain immensely important. We will consider a very different kind of thinking in the next chapter.

8

Thinking Historically

IN THE PREVIOUS chapter I began by contrasting the world of seeing and the world of hearing. The latter is associated especially with Israel. This world of hearing is one form of process thinking. However, I focused on the remarkable denial of substance by an Indian thinker who was never accepted in India but widely adopted in China, Korea, and Japan, where sentences are built around the verb rather than the noun. In these cultures, the emphasis on events supported process thinking but did not develop into historical thinking. This happened only in the world of hearing, and that seems to be primarily found in Israel.

The world of hearing encourages thinking about events and also telling stories about them. To hear meanings involves hearing a flow of sounds, which are heard in their relationship to other sounds. The world of hearing is not what it is in a moment. The moment is an element in a process and would not be what it is if taken out of that process.

The world of vision can hardly include the world of hearing. It contains no meanings or values. As our universities organize their teaching and research in academic disciplines that strive to get back to the world of vision in a pure form, they take pride in being free from values. On the other hand, the world of hearing can include the world of vision as an often useful abstraction from the real world, an abstraction that contributes much that the world of hearing, left to itself, would never attain.

More should be added from the worlds of touch, of taste, and of smell. Still more should be added from the world of nonsensory perception and the world of memory. Both the world of sight and the world of hearing are drastically limited. The claim that heirs of the Bible and its world of hearing can make is that it is more welcoming of its own expansion.

When we think of the external world as consisting primarily of persons like ourselves, with whom we interact, we can generalize downward to animals and plants and atoms and quarks and photonic occasions. In the process, such things as thought and consciousness and even life will drop off, but what we find are still entities that take account of their environments and play a role in constituting themselves. We will not think of a stone as having these characteristics, but we will understand that the ultimate constituents of the stone, the quantum events, do. The atoms may still show traces of this kind, but the stone is put together in a way that eliminates these characteristics from importance. The question is not so much how life emerged in an inanimate world, but how inorganic entities emerged in a world designed for life.

The preceding chapters are examples of thinking historically. Thinking historically leads to understanding that different languages encourage different philosophies. I argued that we who speak Indo-European languages are currently allowing ourselves to be blocked from understanding the world adequately by limiting ourselves to the world of sight.

One thing from which speakers of Indo-European languages are blocked is the process thinking encouraged by languages that focus on events or happenings. This differs quite radically from modern Western scientific thinking. It understands scientific thinking historically and affirms it. But too many scientists, because they no longer know how to think historically, are arguing that scientific thinking alone has a place in education. This is catastrophic.

We have seen that process thinking can make possible a coherent understanding of the natural world and the implications of current findings in the sciences. It can also lead to explaining what is happening by telling stories. Storytelling can expand into an increasingly inclusive explanation of what happens. Then it becomes historical thinking.

Thinking historically does not necessarily mean thinking more about the past. Rather, as it focuses on the present, it understands how the present situation has grown out of past events. Those who lack historical consciousness are apt to view what they experience in the present as simply the way the world has been and will be. Historical thinking understands that much of the way things are came about because of particular historical events, and "the way things are" can be changed by acting historically.

For example, I have argued that when Jesus said the divine commonwealth is at hand, he was saying that the patterns of thinking and organizing and acting common among his fellow Jews were not the only possibility. When one saw that they were leading the Jews toward the destruction of Israel, other patterns could be chosen.

I am writing this on Earth Day. I was asked to write a short piece about that. I thought we could understand Earth Day better if we set it in a history of "isms." I propose that we identify what is of fundamental importance to communities and cultures and then define them accordingly. I suggest that from the Fall of Rome until the middle of the seventeenth century, the West was committed to, and focused on, Christianity. People called themselves Christians and went, voluntarily, at great personal sacrifice, to the Holy Land to take it away from Muslims. The church was more powerful than secular rulers and looked to, by them, to settle issues. Since devotion was directed to Christianity and Christendom rather than to God and Jesus, I say the real religion of the period was Christianism, not Christianity

The Treaty of Westphalia (1648) ended a thirty-year war begun over disputes between Catholics and Protestants. It was concluded that secular rulers would decide which church would be established in their territories. This symbolized and embodied the shift of dominance from church to state, from Christianism to nationalism. Subsequently, millions of people willingly gave their lives for the glory of their nations.

With the Industrial Revolution, nations became very concerned about their national economies. Adam Smith wrote about the wealth of nations. But at the end of the Second World War the nations of Europe decided they had had enough of nationalism. They could all be more prosperous if they cooperated in a community of nations. The wealth they sought was not so much that of the nations but of individuals and of corporations. For the sake of the economy, European nations gave up some of their sovereignty. In the world as a whole, nations began to serve the great transnational corporations. There was a shift from patriotism to attaining individual wealth, from nationalism to economism.

Of course, Christianism did not disappear when national feeling became more important than religious identification. And national feeling continues to be very extensive and very powerful, even though national governments now serve corporations more than they control them. We are now in a world committed to the primacy of wealth.

We are currently seeing the results of this shift in Ukraine. The Russian government seeks to defend itself from the threat of allowing its enemies to establish bases close to its borders. Russians who may support this goal are not willing personally to fight for it. Putin knew that a draft would greatly reduce support for the war. European people in general would strongly resist being drafted. The United States experienced the end of American nationalism in the Vietnam War. This contrasts with Russian-speaking residents of Ukraine, who have been fighting against the nationalistic Ukrainian government since 2014, and with the willingness of Ukrainians to give their lives for their country.

Perhaps economism has not yet reached its zenith. Still, it is clear that economism will end fairly soon. The worship of money is destroying the Earth, and that means that it is unsustainable. Its collapse may end up being the collapse of civilization and even of the human race. But the alternative is clear. If we decide that the economy should serve the Earth rather than destroy it, the new age will be Earthist. We know already what would be involved. There are many obstacles, but they could be overcome. Earthism is at hand.

Understanding cultures in this way helps us to see that the call to serve the Earth is not crazy or hopeless. It is certainly radical. Tinkering with the remnants of nationalism and with current economistic structures and practices will not suffice. There must be a deep spiritual change, and that is already occurring. There are already millions of people who think that life is more important than money. The change is happening. Perhaps it is too slow to save us, but there is hope. The Divine Commonwealth, an ecological civilization—what I am here calling Earthism—is not impossible. We know what to do. The problem is that the media, the governments, most of the schools, and of course the world of business are controlled by the worshippers of money, that is, those whose decisions are made in terms of money and not life.

Historical thinking provides a helpful understanding of where we are and what we need to do. One reason that it is difficult to get a hearing for the importance and the possibility of change in contemporary society is that historical thinking is little emphasized or appreciated in our time. It may be that we need to use historical thinking to show the importance and value of historical thinking.

Before using historical thinking to talk about what is possible and urgently needed, it is well to make ourselves more conscious of what we are doing. Since the Bible is the major, almost the only, source of historical thinking in world history, and since Christians in the past kept it an important part of Western intellectual life, it may be especially important for us who want to be authentic Christians to sharpen our understanding and our practice. Perhaps an illustration of how its presence or absence determines opinions on a current debate in the United States.

The deep disagreement today about who are the "racists" will serve. Some people think "historically." They point out that for centuries, Whites owned Blacks as slaves, treating them simply as property. Blacks could not benefit from their own labor, although it often made their White masters rich. Even when they were legally freed, Blacks were exploited in all sorts of ways, socially, economically, legally, and politically. Especially in the South, the economy was still based on their very poorly paid labor. Their education was designed to keep them in the servant role.

In light of this, special attention now needs to be paid to giving Blacks opportunities to overcome the consequences of this history. Some form of "reparations" should be arranged. Those Whites who oppose reparations are considered "racist." This is the way those who think historically understand racism.

Those dominated by the primacy of sight understand matters differently. They support being blind to race. For them, treating Whites and Blacks differently today is inherently "racist." "Racism" is, by definition, discriminating according to race. When a Black woman is chosen for a position over a White woman because she is Black, that is racist. If we can show that this particular Black woman has been unjustly treated by society and thereby handicapped, giving her the edge might be just. But giving her the edge simply because her ancestors were mistreated is pure racism.

This example shows the difference between historical understanding and dominant forms of modern understanding. In this instance, what "racism" means in historical understanding is ignoring the enormous injustices committed by one race against another race over centuries. In nonhistorical thinking it is allowing race to play a role, positive or negative in treating individuals. When we think historically, we take account of the actual history of racial discrimination and its actual effects on whole communities, largely defined by race. From the nonhistorical perspective, individuals should be treated individually without regard to their race.

Historical thinking has played a large role in the West. This is primarily, almost entirely, due to the influence of the Bible. History plays very little role in the religions of Greece, India, and China, But Judaism and its offspring, Christianity and Islam, have, as their sacred texts, writings about what happened in the past and what is expected in the future. To understand persons or events in the Bible, one must locate them historically and be informed about their historical role.

For example, who was John the Baptist? Some Jews thought he was the Messiah or Christ. When Palestine was part of the Roman Empire, many Jews expected the Messiah or Christ to free them from the Roman yoke. Jesus' followers thought that he, not John, was the Messiah, and that John came to prepare the way for him. Neither of them succeeded in overthrowing the Romans, but in Jesus' case, at least, he made it clear that his proposal for saving Israel was not the military victories that most would-be Messiahs had attempted, but a different way to live and to relate to the Romans.

Much of what Jesus taught could be appropriated even in the context of military defeat and the final expulsion of Jews from Palestine. Indeed, it could be appropriated by Gentiles and reshaped into a very different history. But its primary focus was on dealing with a specific historical issue. Even when the specific historical purpose was lost, Jesus brought with him into the Greco-Roman world the Hebrew scriptures, and the new audience located Jesus as the center of new history. Today the whole world locates itself temporally in relation to Jesus' birth, which is taken as the beginning of new global historical epoch. Despite the enculturation of Jesus' followers into an ahistorical world, Jesus brought historical thinking with him.

A modern person may certainly question the factual basis of the stories the Hebrews told themselves about their heritage. Much of the tradition does not hold up well under such examination. Sometimes, we use the word "historical" in contrast to "mythological." What in the Hebrews' story can be counted as historical in this sense is endlessly discussed.

For example, the state of Israel now wants to base some of its territorial claims on David's kingdom. It has been keenly disappointed that there is very little historical evidence for any such kingdom. This is important, but I am not using "historical" in this modern sense. By the understanding of "historical" in this chapter, if what people think happened in the past is important for them in the present, their consciousness is "historical."

From my perspective, factual accuracy is also of great importance. In this respect, excellent work was done in the nineteenth and early twentieth centuries. Much of it focused on the biblical story, but it also sought to create an overall vision of history that took the rest of the world into account. In that period the university prided itself on its historical research as much as on its scientific research.

I have explained that the growing prestige of the natural sciences ended this period. The telling of stories, even when one works for increasing accuracy, did not measure up well against the accurate predictions produced by scientific thinking. Its status and role in the university reduced dramatically. Few students learn much about scholarly historical method and about how historical knowledge is needed to supplement scientific information.

While departments of history declined in size and number, and what was left often tried to learn about the past through quasi-scientific methods, de-historicization was also occurring elsewhere. For example, scientists became less interested in the history of science. This reduced their ability to consider what they were doing in a critical way.

Nevertheless, there were two fields of study that engaged in serious and detailed historical study. These resulted from powerful movements in the wider culture that brought irresistible pressure to bear on the university. I refer to Black studies and Women's studies. Within them, studies of the past designed to trace the story of their oppression encouraged rigorous and passionate historical work.

They have given birth to changed ways of understanding American history, and world history as well. Currently, a history that is at least partly written from the Black perspective is offered for teaching in public schools. That how we understand ourselves historically is still important is evident in the public response. Several states have forbidden the use of such texts in public education.

It is clear that historical thinking is not disappearing from the university. But I fear there is little teaching about how to evaluate different stories that are in competition. My complaint is that historical thinking is not thematized. Historical methods are not critically evaluated. Most graduates are hardly better prepared to evaluate what they read about current events than are those who do not go to college.

Where there are multiple stories about what has happened, we often must decide which to follow. Consider the competing stories about the role of Trump in the rioting in the capitol. The congressional committee investigating this event is constructing a story that implicates Trump in politically unacceptable activity. Trump and his followers tell a story that presents Trump as innocent. Much of Trump's future role in the American government will be affected by the national decision about which story to believe.

I wish that we could look to our universities for guidance, that there would be experts in guiding people to historical truth. As it is, the decision will not be made on the basis of a serious desire to learn the truth. Unfortunately, the likelihood is that the success of each story will be more influenced by the outcome of midterm elections than by critical reflection. If the Republicans win both houses of Congress, the successful story will be the one that exonerates Trump. The Democrats hope for the victory of a story that condemns Trump. The decision may be delayed for some time. The American future is at stake.

My point is that not long ago there were historians who could tell us how they decide among the different stories about events with which they are constantly confronted. In the nineteenth and early twentieth centuries our universities accepted responsibility for helping us decide what probably happened. Of course, this is an unending task, and historians were often wrong. But there was real improvement.

Sadly, today, the university has largely closed the door on efforts to improve historical understanding. What story will shape the future in the example I have given will probably be determined by who controls what politically. Truth now seems to be irrelevant to success. And the university takes no responsibility for helping society to engage well in historical thinking. It teaches that scientific thinking alone is reliable.

Why the university has abandoned responsibility for truth about what is now going on is an important question that is not discussed in the university or in the church or anywhere else. Since our understanding of what happens historically is so important for what happens in the future, somebody should ask these questions. I would love to think that the Western religions, rooted in Hebrew historical thinking, could be counted on for concern for historical truth. But thus far, they have given no such indications. The liberal Protestants who did much of the relevant historical work in previous centuries are preoccupied with giving comfort.

The realization that most of what we think about current events is determined by factors irrelevant to truth is disturbing. That the university is opposing consideration of historical truth is also disturbing. That the heirs of Israel's historical thinking don't care is disappointing. I will offer an historical explanation of how this situation came about so soon after universities contributed so magnificently to historical understanding. You may disagree with the story I tell. My account is certainly incomplete. But I hope you will be convinced that it is a mistake for universities to silence discussion of this whole topic.

So how did it happen? First, in the sixteenth century, a few students of the natural world decided that the interest of so many scientists in discovering the function of things was distracting them from the deeper question of the efficient causes of things. For example, many scientists were satisfied that they understood the heart when they discovered what it does for the circulation of blood and how its functioning is crucial for animal life. This left them with explanations in the sphere of final causes.

The "modern" scientists rightly saw that much more could be learned by focusing on efficient causes, which they thought were modeled in machines. The clock fulfills its function because it is mechanically designed to do so. We need to understand the mechanisms by which the heart fulfills its function. Modern science organized itself to study efficient causes. Its worldview was that all nature was clocklike.

This mechanical nature was given for and to human beings,

or human minds, which were assumed to be very different from machines. For two centuries the modern West was radically dualistic. The human mind was assumed to be entirely different from nature. Historical thinking retained its importance in thinking about human beings.

Practically speaking, this dualism is still deeply rooted in the dominant Western treatment of nature. But evolutionary theory forced scientists to give up this notion that, fundamentally, human beings are outside of, or above, nature. The implication was that human behavior was also completely determined by physical causes.

The absence of any human self-determination, and therefore of any responsibility for what we do, is the clear implication of what is taught in the university, I have yet to meet any professor who really accepts that idea. In general, professors who hold to deterministic positions are just as critical of those who make bad choices as are others. None seem to think that their own moment by moment choices are irrelevant.

Consciously, or not, Immanuel Kant seems to have won. He distinguished practical reason from pure reason. Pure theoretical reason understands everything to be determined by efficient causes. There is no personal freedom or responsibility. But practical reason operates in an entirely different sphere. This radical dualism has replaced the dualism of humanity and nature. But in the university context all academic disciplines operate entirely in the sphere of pure theoretical reason. That there is another sphere is taken for granted in practice but not relevant in theory.

Even after scientists in principle claimed that their methods and worldview could and should include human beings, universities continued to house humanities that operated in a very different way. History belonged to the humanities. What historians found most interesting were unique events. Some would say that all human events are unique; so, we could say they focused on the unique aspects of what happens. However, the assumption that human beings should be understood as part of nature gradually eroded the independence of the humanities and their freedom to ignore the scientific method and worldview.

In principle, science cannot deal directly with what is unique as such. For science, what appears to be unique is assumed to be explained by actions that are repeatable, but perhaps uniquely related, in a particular event. Its worldview requires that a unique event is an inevitable consequence of deterministically operating causes in a different conjunction. In so far as it is to be studied scientifically, it is reduced to what is repeatable.

Historians operating out of historical consciousness try to find the most accurate story they can in which to locate and understand the event. When students of past events approach these events "scientifically," they look for repeatable patterns that occur under repeatable circumstances. They find them. They may help historians to tell an accurate story. But they cannot tell a story or discuss the methods used by historians in discerning what is more accurate.

As Western culture has become more secular, and the Bible has been excised from its self-understanding, universities have become less tolerant of means of attaining truth other than the scientific one. Of course, there are still some "historians" in the biblical sense, but I'm not sure that there are any graduate departments of history that emphasize the importance and unpredictability of unique events and study how they are to be understood and explained

Which position should we take on "racism"? Which story about the January 6 riot should we believe? So far as the university is concerned, suit yourself. Reason is irrelevant.

Outside of the university, and even in professional schools within the university, stories are still told and evaluated. In a court of law, sometimes everything is settled by discovering who pulled the trigger. But often there are other questions that make a great difference. Was it intentional? Did the person who pulled the trigger do it in self-defense? Was he or she drugged against his or her will? The lawyers draft competing stories, both including the agreed-on pulling of the trigger. The university may no longer give credence to any attempt to judge between stories. But the judging will continue in courts of law and in daily life.

Thus far I have told a story that explains why universities are no longer interested in getting stories as straight as possible. They are committed to a science that does not allow for radical uniqueness or for personal responsibility. This science has been brilliantly successful. It has also narrowed the scope of acceptable thinking in unjustifiable ways. That the liberal Protestant church gives so much more authority to the university than to the Bible is regrettable. We need history as well as science.

Let's suppose some of us decided that, as heirs of the Bible, we would shape our lives around history. We would want first to understand our historical situation as well as possible. We would then ask, given that understanding, and given one's own circumstances and abilities, to what are we called? And, of course, if one is a part of a community that would understand, its help and advice would be invaluable.

But, at least in my view, our calling is not decided only rationally. If we are open to God, things can happen in unanticipated ways. Neither John the Baptist nor Jesus is depicted as focusing on spiritual disciplines. But both of them spent time alone in the wilderness to reflect before God about their vocations.

One's calling is not simply a matter of one's job, although jobs were once called vocations and should be understood that way again. Within any job there are opportunities and choices. One may also be in position to serve in volunteer programs. Sometimes one changes jobs. One retires. At every point, indeed, in every moment, one is called.

Our calling is deeply personal, but it is not limited to personal affairs. God calls all of us to take what responsibility we can for the Earth. The threat to which we are responding is the worst that has occurred since the rise of civilization. Many who sense its seriousness are deciding not to have children. Perhaps that is their calling. Surely others are called to procreate.

Thus far, the only responses to global threats that are seriously discussed are ones that do not require economic sacrifices. A rising price for gasoline is political poison for whoever is in power, and certainly no one would dare to propose it as a way of discouraging driving. Our current economic wellbeing remains the primary concern of the American public. The immediate responsibilities to family and friends make it very difficult to discuss the changes that are needed.

If, in desperation, we turn to the Bible, it will be because we are ready for deeper changes. Maybe we are ready to hear that we cannot serve both God and money. Maybe some of us will choose God.

9

Why Whitehead?
Inclusive Vision

THE PRECEDING CHAPTER calls for a recovery of historical thinking. We need to understand how we got ourselves into such great difficulties and to identify the inherited ideas and customs that must be changed. Historical thinking enables us to identify the possibilities that are at hand. I want people to understand that philosophy has thought itself into a dead end, and that there are saving possibilities at hand. This chapter will bring historical thinking to bear on philosophy, and locate Whitehead's potential historical role.

I have made clear my indebtedness to Whitehead on several topics. But his actual importance for me and his potential importance in the history of thought go far beyond particular achievements. The previous chapter explains historical thinking, and in this chapter, I want to locate Whitehead in the history of Western thought. My thesis is that he has made possible a kind of thinking that late modernity had rejected and largely ended. The needed wholistic response to the desperate dangers we face will not occur without the kind of inclusive vision Whitehead offers.

Much of this chapter will consist of showing how modern philosophy has thought itself into a tiny corner. In that corner it can hardly consider the life-or-death issues faced by humanity, much less help in responding to them. That does not prevent people from forming opinions about these questions, it just leaves these opinions uncriticized. For example, economists often state their understanding of human beings and their behavior. They depict culture as competition among selfish individuals. This is a philosophical question. The Greeks offered much better answers. But philosophers today will only explain why philosophy has nothing to say about this. Rather naïve opinions that shape historical events cannot be critically evaluated in the university.

I will then show how Whitehead offers better answers to the issues that led to philosophy's impotence. He shows how philosophers can examine their experience more carefully and accurately. They may once again throw light on all the most important issues and give urgently needed guidance. They can certainly offer a better starting point for economic thought. What Whitehead offers is not an improved version of what is now understood to be professional philosophy. Like Descartes and Kant, he offers a fresh start in the whole enterprise of philosophical thinking.

In all civilizations there have been thoughtful people who pursued wisdom. So, one can find philosophy in the broad sense of the love of wisdom everywhere. However, in most cultures the thinking is to advance some interest. Confucius wanted to improve the quality of human communities. The Vedantist thinkers of ancient India wanted to understand themselves and transform themselves. That these efforts are different from Western philosophy does not make them more or less valuable.

What Socrates introduced to Athens was the disinterested pursuit of understanding of important questions generally. He wanted to pursue truth simply for the sake of truth. This is to be distinguished from the disinterested understanding of a limited topic. The disinterested study of chemicals is the science of chemistry. The disinterested study of economic phenomena is economics. In this chapter, I am going to limit "philosophy" to the disinterested quest for unspecialized truth. We will then understand that philosophy is one kind of reflection alongside others, and that it arose in only one place, namely, Athens.

The appeal to aim at truth for truth's sake arose as a criticism of the sophists. The sophists were people who offered to teach ambitious citizens of Athens to speak more persuasively in support of whatever policy or individual they sought to support. The sophists were not concerned with expressing their personal opinions about the issues. What they taught would be useful for gaining support for whatever goal was in mind.

Socrates thought that more important than skill in debate was the goal to be sought. What is the best goal can be decided only by reflection of a quite different sort. One needs to understand the world and what life should be directed toward. To be guided by that understanding should be the goal of debate in the public forum. Philosophy is disinterested in the sense that its quest for truth is not distorted by personal preferences or profits. It is, of course, deeply motivated by the desire for truth.

The disinterested reflection across a broad range of matters took a particular form in Athens. Its achievements were impressive. For philosophers, the freer they were from the assumptions of a particular culture or religion, the better. Viewed with historical consciousness, we see that the emergence of philosophy is possible only under specific conditions and that the content and style are in fact affected by particular features of the culture, however hard the philosophers attempt to transcend that. When the culture changes, it may or may not be possible for philosophy to continue.

In the Western European case, cultural change made continuation impossible. In the Roman Empire, a different way of thinking arose. Over several centuries, the majority of people were persuaded that profound and ultimately important beliefs were grounded in historical events through which the true human situation was revealed—as was the nature and call of God.

For these people, to continue to pursue philosophy by setting aside what had been learned through historical events would be foolish. The most reflective persons will think about what has already been learned and how to relate that to other matters. This we can call "theology." People who trusted Jesus' message and what his followers had taught about him did not pretend to give up all that and reflect without preexisting convictions.

When the empire in the West collapsed, or we might say, when it continued only in the form of the church, there was no longer any place for philosophy. Nevertheless, leading theologians found the work of some philosophers to be very helpful. St. Augustine provided a theology richly informed by philosophy. For a thousand years pure philosophy was replaced by philosophical theology.

I consider myself to be a philosophical theologian. I believe that what I have learned from Israel, for example, to think historically, is not something to be set aside so as to be purely philosophical. I think we should begin with what we have in fact already learned in the course of history. My view is that with regard to the existentially most important issues, Jesus' teaching and life are of supreme importance for me. I reflect as a disciple of Jesus. As a disciple of Jesus, I find Whitehead's philosophy immensely helpful.

Sadly, power passed from the secular rulers of the empire to the political rulers of the church. In the process, questions never imagined by Jesus divided Roman Christians. Creeds were affirmed and enforced to maintain the unity of the institution. The church required that the thinking of Christians conform to these. In my view, putting creeds forward as absolute requirements enforced politically was a profound betrayal of Jesus. It certainly limited and damaged philosophical theology.

For philosophy to reappear, the church had to lose control of intellectual life. This control was challenged from time to time, but the real break came with the Protestant Reformation. This time, whole sections of the church broke away. The reformers persuaded many, even many who stayed in the Catholic church, that there are alternatives. Some individuals felt the need to consider more than one. The door was open to philosophy. It was a Catholic who stepped through.

In the seventeenth century, René Descartes was very clear that we should not begin with accepting the authority of any established institution. The question we must ask of them is how they came to their conclusions. We also need to find a starting point on which all can agree. This will allow us to pursue the quest for truth rationally, without interference of political power. That is, it will reestablish pure philosophy.

Of course, in historical perspective, we see that Descartes' thinking was deeply affected by his historical/cultural context. The goal of renewing philosophy was a new possibility in his day. And the way he found to counter the authority of revelation itself grew out of just that revelation. Historical thinking emphasizes both the enormous role of history in shaping new developments and the role of those new developments in reshaping history.

In this case, Descartes proposed that philosophy should start by examining one's personal experience. This is the one indubitable reality for each of us. For Descartes, the renewal of philosophy was possible by affirming that "I think, therefore, I am." Centuries of Christian self-examination separate classical philosophy from this new beginning. This starting point has made modern philosophy very different from classical philosophy.

Of course, a great deal of reflection went on independent of this extreme anthropocentric individualism. The natural sciences focused on the world we experience, with little or no attention to how a human being experiences it. Many turn to psychology in order to understand themselves. Philosophy does not set the stage for all thinking. Nevertheless, Descartes has been extremely important for modern Western thought.

The meaning of "I" in the phrase "I exist" is philosophically crucial. Descartes meant that there was a subject of thinking and existing that could also do other things. He understood the "I" about whose existence he could be certain as a substance. Buddha had directly rejected this view, but Greek philosophy and medieval philosophical theology had not produced an alternative. At least implicitly, Descartes could assume without dispute, that to be is to be substantial. If there was thinking, there had to be something that thought, and that meant, something substantial.

The most important thinkers who took up Descartes' call to base beliefs on actual individual experience were the British empiricists. They pressed the question of what in experience gives us information about the external world, the world studied by science. They concluded that only the sense organs did this.

This conclusion followed from the understanding of the "I" as substantial. It is obvious that our experience in any moment is not constituted entirely by sense experience. There is, in addition, at least memory. But the data of memory can be viewed as the earlier experience of the same I. Thus, the distinction remains between the experience of the I and the experience of the world external to the I. The latter seemed to be limited to the sense organs.

Elsewhere I have pointed out that, for all practical purposes, speakers of the Indo-European languages limited themselves to sight. This intensified the problem and distorted the analysis of what is learned from other senses. Sight locates its data, patches of color, in the distance. In so far as modern philosophers have taken account of senses other than sight, they have applied to them the model derived from sight and described their data simply as phenomena.

David Hume was the first to draw the conclusions of this starting point. He wanted to ground modern science firmly in empirical experience. Central to modern science is the idea that everything can be explained by efficient causes. He sought the experience of such causality in vision and could not find it. He was distressed.

The net result of reflection based on the experience of a substantial "I," limited to sense experience of the external world, was to undercut the possibility of the inclusive vision anticipated by Descartes. We are shut into ourselves and the data of our sense experience. That data is limited to appearances or phenomena. Causality cannot be a phenomenon. It was Immanuel Kant who developed this understanding with great detail and rigor. It puts an end to realism, often called "naïve" realism. The philosophy that has given up the goal of knowledge of an external world is very limited indeed.

Kant is thoroughly Cartesian in beginning with individual human experience. But the change is very marked. Descartes' goal was to develop a reliable understanding of the real world in which we live and which science studies. Kant was asking what philosophy can do, now that we realize our knowledge of the external world is restricted to the data of our senses, that is, to phenomena.

I now think that the change in philosophy effected by Kant requires that we consider him, like Descartes, as a new beginning. The topics are different. The goal is different. We can speak of three periods of Western philosophy: the classic, the Cartesian, and the Kantian.

Of course, from graduate school days I knew that Kant was important. I was personally keenly interested in whether God exists and what we can know about the divine nature. I was convinced that these were the right questions for me to ask. But

I found that, even in a very open school of theology, directly asking them was not easy. I became increasingly aware that Kant had influenced religious thought, including Christian theology, so as to discourage ontological questions. I saw that my beliefs required speculation, since they went far beyond phenomenological description, and I wrote my doctoral dissertation to show that the effort to avoid speculation in forming a theology was virtually hopeless. But even then I did not fully appreciate that it was Kant I was struggling with.

When I began to teach theology, I saw that the process theology with which I identified was viewed askance by most professionals, whereas lay people often found it attractive. I realized that professional theology, like professional philosophy, was trying to keep to the boundaries established by Kant. But I also saw that the resulting disconnection between Christian theology and Christian faith was damaging the progressive church. Confusion about "God" does not evoke wholehearted commitment.

Nevertheless, I was startled when teaching at the University of Mainz by a gradual student's question. I had been invited to teach there by Wolfhart Pannenberg who was interested in process theology, although definitely not an adherent. The question was whether Whitehead was a "critical thinker."

I had been expounding him and did not understand how anyone could consider him uncritical. But that was not the question. To be truly "critical" meant that one accepted Kant's masterpiece, *The Critique of Pure Reason*, as the place to begin. My questioner thought one should be critical in this sense and otherwise had no right to be teaching in a university. He reflected the dominant view. By this meaning, Whitehead is not a critical thinker.

I realized that this was the reason he was so little taught in American universities, as well. What he was doing was not allowed by Kant. Like the early moderns, Whitehead wanted to know about the nature of the real world.

Whitehead, in fact, was more like the Greeks. One could start anywhere. He was a mathematical physicist, and he could start with questions about the ontological status of mathematical objects or the nature of quanta. But he could also start with immediate personal experience.

When he did so, he understood that what we have with Descartes' "cogito" can be analyzed into a series of events. These events are very brief, perhaps a sixth of a second in duration. Each is a synthesis of the past. In the case of human experiences, a long line of previous experiences plays a primary role. But the synthesis includes thousands of occurrences within the body and many external to it. For the most part, an experience is determined by the past out of which it comes, but just how it puts things together is its own decision.

For the Cartesians, the external world was the world external to the substantial "I." For Whitehead it is the world preexisting the new occasion. The Cartesian external world plays no role in constituting the substantial "I." The Whiteheadian external world, that is, the past, largely constitutes the newly becoming experience. The past flows into the present.

Whitehead calls the sensory experience featured by Cartesians "presentational immediacy." He largely agrees with Kant about this experience. But foundational to every experience is the past world that is flowing into it. This relation is not mediated by the senses. He calls it perception in the mode of "causal efficacy" or nonsensory perception.

I am proposing that we recognize, for professional philosophy and also theology, that Kant's *Critique of Pure Reason* has reshaped the philosophical task. It is better to refer to the book than the thinker. The thinker was equally interested in morality, but his influence in that area today is modest. His third critique, the one on judgment, seems to break out of the restrictions announced in the first, but it is rarely read.

From the late eighteenth century to the present, the followers of the first critique have been remarkably creative and diverse. In Germany, in the nineteenth century, they created what we call German idealism. When reflection about the natural world was thought to be impossible, philosophers studied the mental and spiritual world and expanded historical thinking about it.

However, other thinkers questioned the possibility of knowing about the subjective experience of past thinkers and focused on what is immediately accessible. Phenomenology and existentialism became dominant in the early twentieth century. But even they fell before deconstructive postmodernism. The fundamental negations about theoretical reason in the first critique lend themselves better to deconstruction than to positive affirmations.

In the English-language world, the Austrian thinker Ludwig Wittgenstein has dominated the philosophical scene in the twentieth century and on into the twenty-first. He directed attention away from thought and subjective experience to linguistic analysis. Much of interest has been learned, especially from the founder of the school, but this philosophy seems self-enclosed, as one interesting topic among hundreds that are considered in the university.

Whitehead is a problem for professional philosophers and theologians. They have gone to great lengths to limit what they talk about. What do they do with someone who thinks what they are omitting is important and talks a lot about it? In some instances, these people can simply be dismissed as "pre-critical." But Whitehead understood Kant well. He is clearly post-critical. What to do?

For a long time, the answer was simple: ignore and exclude. But around the edges of university discourse there were always a number of people dissatisfied with its restrictions and limitations. Some of them found Whitehead interesting. Most important, as the environmental crisis became imminent, it was embarrassing to some academics that they had avoided the topic. Whitehead's followers had not, and others have become interested in what we had been doing.

Continental Europeans have recently opened their doors to Whitehead. It has become possible to study Whitehead in a number of continental universities. American universities seem interested, but they still have no place for the study of his thought.

My interpretation of the situation is that Whitehead's philosophy is offering itself as another major turning point comparable to Descartes and Kant. Whitehead's understanding of the role of philosophy, to provide a coherent, inclusive vision, is a return to classical philosophy and to Descartes, but he shows that until substance thinking is overcome, the goal cannot be realized. He shares the focus on subjective human experience, but he shows that it consists in events. He opens the door to reflection about how the natural world is constituted, and he seeks to correct the philosophical beliefs of most scientists.

Whitehead lays the framework for renewing coherent comprehensive thinking. He does so by offering a model. He does not only say that philosophy can enable science to contribute to an inclusive vision. He works out just how that can be done.

Comprehensive thinking must include mathematics and logic. That was Whitehead's specialty. *Principia Mathematica* is a major landmark in the history of reflection in those fields. Comprehensive thinking must include science. Whitehead worked extensively on general relativity, coming up with a formula that produces exactly the same results as Einstein's but without the mystification and unintelligibility. He preferred a formula whose predictions differed very slightly from Einstein's. Thus far, it has received no support from empirical studies, but it is available in case even more refined measures do lead to the need for change.

Whitehead's philosophy is already recognized as fitting better with empirical information about the quantum world. He can provide an understanding not only of that world but also of how

it relates to the world of physical "mass" that constitutes the preferred topic of mainstream physics. And he can interpret it all in a
way that treats life nonreductively. He shows that much of science's
inability to formulate its manifold discoveries in a coherent way
comes from its clinging to materialism and mechanism, concepts
that are plausible and useful in a limited range of scientific findings,
but useless with regard to the deepest level of reality.

Whereas the continuing articulation of the mechanistic model
sets up a situation of inevitable tension in the understanding of
human experience, Whitehead's organic, process model does not.
Neuroscience has advanced greatly since Whitehead's day, but the
advance makes it fit better into a Whiteheadian model. These days
there is considerable interest in paranormal and psychedelic experience. This also tends to support what Whitehead wrote. And his
book on religion and his comments on God have had considerable
resonance.

With Whitehead so little regarded in the twentieth century,
those of us who followed him enjoyed projecting a dramatic
change in the twenty-first century. We began to claim that the
shift was beginning. We called our press, the "process century
press." Of course, no one could say that in fact the twenty-first
century is Whiteheadian, but the possibility is becoming visible.
The dominant professional philosophers today have little to offer.
The Kantian traditions have run dry. Of the scattered thinkers
who have independently done creative work, Whitehead stands
out. There is a chance.

The goal of a coherent vision is not an obscure one that needs
complex justification. Most people have multiple views that do not
cohere with one another. But when they see that they are implying
ideas that they do not believe or contradicting themselves, they
are uncomfortable. If someone helps them to put things together
more coherently, they are apt to be pleased.

When people are told that what is false in science is at the same time true in practical life, they may accept it on Kantian authority, and remember to keep their ideas away from science, but it does not really seem right. When people are told that their purposes have no practical outcome, the incoherence is even less acceptable. No people before recent times were schooled to accept such radical incoherence of thought and experience. Thus, Whitehead is siding with very deep assumptions and intuitions in thoughtful people. As they learn that there is no reason to force their minds into incoherence, the Whiteheadian turn may occur with remarkable speed.

Saving the world requires love, and especially love of enemies. It requires us to subordinate decisions about money to goals of overall wellbeing. It calls us to truth and justice for the least of these. Equally, it requires peace among nations and widespread commitment to a living Earth. It requires reforming education and all the other institutions of society.

My most radical statement is the thesis and conclusion of this chapter. It is that if we are to approach our task with sufficient passion and conviction, we need an integrated, inclusive vision that shows us how valuable the life system of the world is. Many people have arrived at some such view by common sense and general experience, their own, and that of their friends. We can work together with them whether or not they know anything about Whitehead.

But the leaders of society, especially through their control of the universities, lock the doors of all the fragmenting academic disciplines to this kind of thinking. They teach generation after generation of "experts" the advantages of tunnel vision. To change this will require the visibility to all, and the ready availability, of an example of coherent, inclusive thinking. Whitehead offers just what is needed. In comprehensiveness and rigor, he has no competition. Why Whitehead? The world needs him. Urgently.

10

What Can We Do in
the United States?

I HOPE all the chapters thus far have helped in various ways to clarify our actual situation. I hope I have showed that just as Jesus called people to work for the divine commonwealth, we can call people to work, under whatever name they wish, for an ecological civilization. And I hope I have shown the importance of historical thinking, indicated how it highlights the importance of Whitehead, and suggested appropriate lines of change for individuals and groups.

I have not said a great deal about the horrors that await us, especially if we do not make major changes. Currently I judge that the United States is the place where changes are most important. In any case, I am an American and feel most responsibility for what my nation does. Accordingly, my focus is on what we are doing and what we need to do in this country. This chapter and the next three make more specific proposals for American Christians to understand what their nation has done and is doing in the world.

To act without knowing what has happened and is happening can often do more harm than good. American Christians have done too much of that. Learning and sharing the truth is already Christian action, and it can pave the way for wise interventions. I have emphasized that historical consciousness is a great gift of Israel, through Jesus and Mohammed, to the world. Preserving it and using it to guide action is part of what we need to do.

We need a more "accurate" story especially about ourselves and our nation. Most stories are told in order to influence their hearers or readers. Some, of course, are avowedly fiction. Fiction can convey truth. But modern historical consciousness is concerned to distinguish true stories from fictional ones. And it quickly learns that much that claims truth is distorted by the interests of the storyteller.

It is also important to recognize that the accuracy of a story does not mean it is the only true story. Many true stories can be told about the same event. If one story claims to be THE truth, one must distrust it. But studying several true accounts can lead to useful judgments of importance. When a writer who tells us some true things about an event is obviously skipping other features of the event intentionally so as to lead to inaccurate impressions, at a deeper level, this "truth" is not true.

I try to read more than one side of important debates. I sometimes find that those who adopt one side, often the popular one, do not respond to the questions raised by critics, but simply repeat a few statements (sometimes accurate ones) and treat the critic as irresponsible for doubting them, or for bringing up facts they do not explain. This has been the case in much of the discussion of responses to Covid. I have followed government recommendations and requirements to support the staff of the retirement home in which I live. But I tend to take the critics as offering a more inclusive truth. If I know the people involved in the debate personally, I have additional grounds for judgment.

I will illustrate all this in relation to what may be the single most important event in recent American history. We call it 9/11, and we remember that on that day, three skyscrapers abruptly collapsed into their own footprints, and that the Pentagon was also attacked. Our government blamed Al Qaeda, and on the basis of this incident became fully engaged militarily in the affairs of the Middle East. Defense Department budgets increased, and the CIA became the most powerful branch of government. The foreign policy supported by the neoconservatives has been in place since then.

Much of this story belongs to the study of how 9/11 was used to justify a foreign policy intent on the United States dominating all the nations of the Earth. We will turn to this and its consequences in the next chapter. But even apart from international consequences, the stories told about the event are extremely important. The official story is that all this was planned and executed by an Islamic organization in Afghanistan, with no help from anyone on the inside of the American government. We are asked to believe that every American official acted correctly, that the recommended procedures were all carried out, and there was nothing wrong with the recommended procedures. Quite amazing.

Church leaders and members alike accepted this story and the implications drawn from it. They did not consider it to be the sort of thing with which the church should concern itself. Events of this kind are "politics," and the church is expected to stay out of politics. Accepting what our duly elected political leaders say is the way to stay out of politics. This is known as being "politically correct," and it is the safest position to adopt. The churches like safety.

You will know that, although I agree that this is the way to stay out of politics, I am quite sure it is not the way to be faithful to Jesus. He did not recommend accepting whatever either the

Roman emperor or the Jewish leaders said. He encouraged his followers to seek the truth and be guided by it.

I know of only one Christian theologian who saw seeking the truth about what happened on Sept. 11 as worthy of a Christian's time. David Griffin was my closest theological associate. I can assure you that he had no illusion that he personally would benefit in any way from seeking and publishing the truth as he uncovered it. He had no motive other than exposing the truth. Truth had special importance in this instance because the United States was justifying many terrible actions on the basis of lies.

Griffin noticed immediately that the official story was improbable. No skyscraper had ever fallen because of fire. According to the government's story, fire brought down three that day. True, we saw the planes crash into two of them. But that explains less than most people suppose. These buildings were built to withstand such crashes. Still, for many people, common sense gave plausibility to this being the cause. However, the third building fell in just the same way as the others. It had not been hit by a plane. And, quite surprisingly, there was discussion of the possibility of the collapse of this building before it occurred. It was even announced by the BBC.

The list of anomalies goes on and on. The challenges to the story were detailed and rigorous. The government's answers were mostly vague and limited. If the government was lying to us about this, David thought that people ought to know. A real investigation was needed. Since the government never engaged in one, David took it on. He gave a decade of his theological life to this examination and to describing the increasing evidence that key leaders in the American government bear primary responsibility.

Of course, major publishers would not publish his books. Church publishers were almost equally opposed. David wrote one book on 9/11 specifically for Christians. Westminster Press had been publishing his theological writings for years, and he persuaded the editors to publish this one also. Sadly, the editors who were responsible were fired. There was no suggestion that the book was mistaken in facts or badly written. It was simply that Westminster Press put political correctness above truth.

The Press did not promote the book, and very few people ever knew of its existence. So far as I know, there were no reviews. It remains the only book telling the truth about 9/11 published by a mainstream press. We should honor the editors for their integrity and courage, but their fate at the hands of the church shows where the church's basic commitments lie.

Of course, David made mistakes. But what is astonishing is how few and relatively minor they are. His books played a role in finally getting professionals to consider what actually happened. Several thousand licensed architects and engineers have now committed themselves to learning and publishing the truth about 9/11.

Architects and Engineers for 9/11 Truth have solid scientific evidence that the official story about the third building, put out by the National Institute of Standards and Technology (NIST), cannot be correct. They have followed standard procedure when government reports need correction and provided the information to NIST, the branch of government called on to produce its account. They have asked NIST to correct its errors. NIST has declined to do so. The architects and engineers have sought a court order. The judge has declined.

What is most interesting is that the judge ruled that although the public has a right to NIST's report, it has no right for that report to be accurate and honest. This is the closest thing I have seen to an acknowledgment that the government is free to lie, and that it has no responsibility to justify doing so. The government is telling us that the fact that it states something is no reason to believe it is true. This is a virtual admission that the accounts the government has provided us of what happened on 9/11, 2001, are false.

The professional architects and engineers who care about truth deserve our support. They are putting truth above popularity and career advancement. But to this day, Christian churches and David's fellow theologians, as a group, have, at best, ignored David's work. That our government has destroyed three buildings, killing hundreds of people, in order to gain support for a highly militarized, imperialist, foreign policy is not considered a matter of interest to Christians.

David's first book on 9/11 is entitled *The New Pearl Harbor*. He took this title from the writings of the neoconservatives who saw that they could not get support from the American public for their new foreign policy without something like what happened at Pearl Harbor.

Roosevelt provoked the Japanese attack on Pearl Harbor in order to end the American public's resistance to getting into World War II. It was clear to David that the neoconservatives successfully engineered 9/11 so as to end resistance to their leadership. Would disciples of Jesus have no interest in such matters? Do Christian have no objection to basing foreign policy on crimes and lies?

Of course, this is just one instance. If it were an exception, if in all other matters we can believe what we are told, it would not deserve the space I have devoted to it. But we have been lied to about Iraq, Syria, and Afghanistan. We are now being lied to about Russia and Ukraine and about China.

Also, the extreme difficulty of publishing what the government does not want published continues. The architects and engineers who know that the official story cannot be true have tried again and again to get *The New York Times* to acknowledge their existence—to no avail. Remember this when you hear Americans condemning China for controlling the flow of information there. China is certainly restrictive. I have many criticisms of China. But Americans who believe in freedom of the press should focus on the CIA control of what is published here before self-righteously critiquing China. Jesus told us to take the beam out of our own eye before criticizing others.

I believe the successful deception of the American people by its government has worked, and is working, strongly against an ecological civilization. The government now knows that with respect to what it does in the rest of the world, we Americans will support whatever it wants us to support. That, on the whole, this fact is simply ignored by all the Christian communities, is a sign of the extent to which nationalism and acculturation in a secular society have triumphed in the churches over Jesus and truth. I dare to think that if we had thought in a biblical way, that is, historically, acquiescence in crimes and lies of this magnitude would not have been so extensive.

Consider a quite different issue that is also of great importance to the future of our country. Partisanship goes with party politics; it has been a feature of American life for a long time. However, in the past, it was often checked by a patriotic sense of the importance of having a working government. Today it seems that some of our leaders are more concerned about promoting their party and weakening the other one than about whether the national government works. There is widespread agreement that this is dangerous for the nation.

The Democrats want to blame this entirely on Trump and his followers. Some of these latter have stated they will oppose anything proposed by Democrats just because it is initiated by Democrats. The invasion of the capitol on June 6 also signaled that the working of government was not a high priority for some of Trump's followers.

However, the anti-Trump Democrats share some of these attitudes. They did what they could to make difficulties for Trump especially in the first two years of his presidency. They worked incessantly to pin something on him with respect to Russia. None of the charges stuck, but they succeeded in making it difficult for him to govern. And those of us who agree with some of his policies, such as moving away from free trade, find it difficult to express our agreements with him in anti-Trump circles. "You are supporting Trump," they say, as if that were an unforgivable sin. Democrats demonize Trump, and Trumpites demonize lots of Democrats, beginning with Biden.

Given this political climate, the prospects of positive leadership toward a world in which God's will is done, an ecological civilization, are dim indeed. Is this important for Christians? Apparently not, if we can judge by the amount of leadership responding to it emanating from the Christian community. The problem is recognized, but it is considered chiefly as it affects congregations and denominations. In general, the response is to stay away from the issues. Often the church's contribution is to "pray about it."

I fear that the extensive use of "prayer," or, more often, talk about the use of prayer, has soured me about what the church calls "prayer." But I believe that real prayer could play a significant role in leadership designed to enable people to work together. Suppose the church seriously taught love of enemy to its members on both sides of the political spectrum. To love your enemy at a minimum will be to seek to understand her or him. Praying together might play a very positive role. And people on both sides will find that much of what they most oppose is opposed by people on the other side as well. If the church became the place where mutual demonization was best overcome, it could offer its services to the nation.

Or suppose the church strongly encouraged its members to reflect together on the nature of a world in which God's will is done, beginning, perhaps, with ideas of ecological civilization. Members would discover that, as individuals, they could share much more than they had supposed and that they could work together based on those agreements.

The fact that the church has taken political correctness and neutrality as its norm rather than seeking that God's will be done does not mean it has made no contribution to an ecological salvation. Jesus makes it clear that every act of kindness, every move toward reconciliation, and every gift that helps to feed the hungry are welcomed. And millions of Christians have engaged in tens of millions of actions through which they help one another and other people. To whatever extent, and I think it is considerable, the church has supported its members in meeting the needs of others, the church contributes to ecological civilization. That should not be denied or minimized.

Also, much of the progressive church has joined secular progressive culture in the dramatic shift away from racism and sexism. Of course, not all the church has taken part. That the varieties of culture are mirrored in the church is another indication that the church as a whole has lost its countercultural moorings. Nevertheless, what was once mainline Protestantism has worked hard to actualize the call for racial and sexual equality. And it has tried to open itself to learning from nonWhites and women. I think, with all its continuing failures, its record of change is commendable. It has certainly contributed to a world in which God's will is done.

There is also one extraordinary achievement of the progressive church led by liberal Protestants that we should celebrate. It has treated its own scriptures with a vivid historical consciousness. In its seminaries, future ministers are taught critical historical understanding of the scriptures from which they preach. Did the events they record actually happen? How are they to be understood in their historical context? How are we to deal with them today? How can we teach our people to understand and appreciate ideas about the past that are not based on facts?

My claim is not only that liberal Protestantism has led in critical study of its sacred writings. It is also that the traditional Protestant clergy are the professionals best informed about the tradition of which they are a part. Protestant clergy know that there is much in their history of which they need to repent. In fact, there is much in the history of the health professionals, the legal professionals, and the educational professionals of which they need to repent. But they are not as well prepared by their education. Many respected members of these professions are largely ignorant of their roles in earlier generations.

Scientists are a special case. For a while a fair number did study the history of modern science in general and of their specialty as well. This frees them to avoid sticking with mistakes made in the past. I have said perhaps too much about this in previous chapters. But since they are the high priests of our day, their loss of interest in history has a particularly disturbing consequence.

We can also note that no nation has been as self-critical as liberal Protestants. Liberal Protestants in the past half century have been exposed to "fundamentalism" much more in their schools than in their churches. Both national histories and sciences have been presented with strong tendencies to fundamentalism. I have found among my Protestant friends an angrier response when I criticize our nation or our universities than when I criticize our churches. Perhaps even as we fade away, we have a role in encouraging self-knowledge and self-criticism in American society.

11

American Foreign Policy from Conquering "Savages" to Global Dominance

WE CANNOT understand ourselves as Americans without understanding how we have related to the rest of the world. In our teaching of American history in our high schools, we are making progress. But we still do not fully appreciate how, from the beginning, relations to others shaped our existence.

Before there was a United States, the colonies flourished at the expense of the indigenous people by stealing their land. They fought the French and Indian wars to keep the process going. The British crown made some attempt to keep the British presence in North America limited to the Atlantic coastal area. One major reason for fighting for independence was to free the colonists to expand indefinitely into indigenous land. George Washington's fortune was dependent on further thefts from the indigenous people. The colonists won, and we have used our freedom from restrictions on Westward expansion to the hilt.

Few of us can read what we did to the earlier inhabitants of the land we conquered without horror. We Euro-Americans justified genocide by the "savagery" of the "injuns." We illustrated their savagery by their practice of scalping. Of course, it turns out that we initiated that practice. A common expression was "No good injun, but a dead injun."

Although we seized the land, we did not want, ourselves, to engage in all the labor required to profit fully from it. So, we bought slaves to do the work. The economy of much of the United States was based on slavery. Before the Civil War, my Cobb ancestors were wealthy Georgians. Of what did their wealth consist? Of land stolen from the indigenous people and the forced labor of enslaved Africans.

Perhaps the most dramatic step in shaping our policies toward Europeans and the rest of the Western Hemisphere was the Monroe Doctrine. We told the European countries to leave, and stay away from, Latin America. It belonged to us. That is, its resources were ours to exploit. We would allow countries to choose their own leaders as long as they were compliant with our interests. The policy was enforced by our army. It was amazingly successful. We exercised unipolar dominance of the Western hemisphere for centuries. Only quite recently have there been successful challenges. The fact that they can now negotiate for help in development with China has opened a new door.

The other side of our policy was to stay out of the quarrels and wars among European nations. In relation to the Eastern hemisphere, until the twentieth century, we tended toward isolationism. We did not establish colonies in Africa or Asia. I grew up feeling that we Americans were more virtuous than the Europeans because we were not "imperialists." I was not encouraged by my schooling to think much about our relation to the "savages" who had inhabited the land on which our nation was built or the Latin Americans we claimed to protect from imperialist Europeans. However, in the first half of the twentieth century, the United States was sucked into two world wars. After the second one, it emerged as the single great power in the world. It had no intention of withdrawing to the Western Hemisphere.

The war against Hitler was fought chiefly on Russian soil. Russian losses were in the tens of millions. Its industry was destroyed. Nevertheless, it won. Although exhausted, it had no intention of being subservient to American capitalism. It continued to practice and to globally promote its Communist ideology.

Communists in China overcame the Western-oriented and capitalist government of Chiang Kai-shek. And Communists were gaining ground, especially among the poor, all over the world. Although the United States was far richer, it felt significantly threatened by Communism and the latter's Russian homeland. Foreign policy was largely one of weakening the appeal of Communism and of the countries that adopted it. We had a dipolar world.

We fought an awful war in Vietnam to stop the spread of Communism. We lost. One difficulty the government had was that we fought primarily with a drafted Army. Armies of that kind had worked well in the two world wars. Most young men were proud to fight for their country. But fighting against peasants struggling for self-determination was different. They did not seem like wicked Communists threatening our nation. Many draftees fought unwillingly. The young people of the country protested against the war. For once, national propaganda did not counterbalance the lived experience of the soldiers. We lost the war.

Never again would the United States depend on the enforced military service of citizens. We would build an Army of professionals. A public not threatened by conscription would pay less attention. The government could fight whom and when it wished without arousing opposition. Public opinion is still critical, but it can be shaped by controlled media. Even if there is some public opposition, it is not intense, since no one is being drafted to fight.

Wars in Iraq, Syria, and Afghanistan have brought little glory to our nation, but the public has not interfered.

Considering our huge defense budget, our record in wars has been remarkably unimpressive. Many of us are suspicious that the money is not spent with military success as the only goal. The defense budget has never been audited properly. Such estimates as have been made indicate that trillions of dollars cannot be accounted for. It is hard not to suspect that some of our billionaires owe much of their fortune to this unaudited budget. It seems to be another example of economism at work. Money comes first. The wellbeing of the nation, even as measured in military terms, is not the government's highest priority.

In contrast to the lackluster performance of the greatest military force the world has ever seen, we used our unique economic strength at the end of World War II with great success. Wall Street became the center of world finance. The reserves of many nations were deposited there. The dollar became the international currency. And our "hit-men" led developing nations to use our money and our corporations in ways that allowed us to exploit their resources, binding them to our will. We still control many votes in the United Nations in these ways.

The economic power of the United States, more than its military power, led to the collapse of Communism as a globally significant alternative to capitalism. The Soviet Union collapsed. Although the Communist party still rules China, it makes no effort to promote Communism elsewhere and no pretense to practice it at home. On the contrary, China is a key contributor to global industrial capitalism.

It is true that, to a greater extent than most capitalist countries, China has worked to eliminate poverty. By establishing itself as the greatest low-cost producer in the world, it has lifted half a billion people from poverty as defined by the United Nations. Some now put the figure at 800 million.

The end of the dipolar world offered a great opportunity for a more peaceful and cooperative world in which the United States could stand out as the great success of democracy and human rights. The United States still has, among many people, an image that connects to this vision. In many countries, there are still idealists who want their countries to become more like the United States.

I have a correspondent in Ukraine. I am trying to persuade him that the sooner Ukraine makes peace with Russia, the better for Ukraine. The United States opposed negotiations before Russia's invasion and immediately after. In the summer of 2022 negotiations in Turkey between Ukraine and Russia nearly succeeded. Prime Minister Boris Johnson of Great Britain, America's closest ally, went to Kiev to redirect Ukraine away from a negotiated settlement. The United States rightly judges that a protracted war will advance its anti-Russian goals. I am trying to get my friend to oppose the United States on this point for the sake of the people of Ukraine. But he is profoundly reluctant to think ill of the United States.

It is somewhat ironic that my strongest critics in China are young people who want China to become more like the United States. They consider me far too cooperative with the Chinese government.

This continuing belief in the United States as the bastion of democracy and human rights could have undergirded American leadership toward a peaceful and democratic world. Despite all that I have said critically about American foreign policy, I recognize that the United States has sometimes acted well on the international scene.

I was in the U.S. Army of Occupation in Japan after World War II. Our treatment of our defeated enemy was a model that should be widely admired and emulated. Japan's pacifist constitution has been a great asset in overcoming the fear of Japan that its behavior had evoked. Breaking up the great concentrations of economic power improved the Japanese economy and led it to serve the people more effectively. The government became more responsive to the people. And, in Japan, the United States has a great ally. Taking our great values as our guide benefited the world, including our country.

However, the goodwill that our leadership in Japan and at other times and places has evoked has lessened as we give up on persuading and depend on our military and economic power more often to compel obedience. Some thirty countries are now sanctioned by the United States. Sanctions do not evoke love. Those countries and others may still obey us, but only because they are forced to do so. When there are other options, such support will end.

A better world was "at hand." But the United States rejected that possibility. The global victory of capitalism over communism did not end the Western enmity toward Russia and China. This is because of a profound change in the goals of the United States already noted in the preceding chapter. By organizing 9/11, neoconservatives gained control of the foreign policy of the United States. They want a world with a single controlling center supporting the growth and ever-increasing profits of the great transnational corporations. They see the United States as the only possible leader.

The dominant corporations after World War II were American, but now they are joined by others, and most of them have become transnational. In this vision, the goal is for the United States to provide the financial and military support for these transnational corporations to flourish. Whereas most countries could not be relied on to govern such a world, "American exceptionalism" assures us that the United States will use its global dominance for the benefit of the world.

This kind of thinking had been more Republican than Democratic. In the United States, the Democratic Party had been heavily based in organized labor after World War II. It would not have continued to have labor union support if it forced workers to compete with those in poorer countries. However, some saw that it was losing to the Republican Party, which was heavily based in business. The Democratic Party shifted to support of transnational business. Bill Clinton led in this move and rammed through Congress an agreement, NAFTA (North American Free Trade Agreement), that made it possible for productive facilities to move to Mexico and sell their products in the United States. The Democrats led in working on other trade agreements with Asia and Europe. In the United States, industrial labor unions were destroyed. Indeed, the workers, who had achieved middle class status, were thrown back into poverty. Many working-class people want America to be great again.

Transnational corporations want to be free to obtain resources anywhere, at any time, to produce where it costs them the least, and to sell where they can get the best price. According to economic theory, this is "efficiency," and it will produce the best products at the lowest prices. The global economy overall will grow, benefiting all. Those who have accepted the dominant economic theory as the guide to truly rational, and therefore "good," behavior, are confident that this goal of a global market controlled by the United States is worth whatever it costs. Of course, it holds down wages and makes the organization of industrial labor almost impossible. It also means that it is hard for countries to protect themselves from pollution, or their natural resources from exploitation. It concentrates wealth in fewer and fewer hands.

Writing in December of 2022, I have come to recognize that the United States will probably be successful in achieving unipolar dominance. For a decade or so China seemed to be rising while U.S. dominance was slipping. Since China and Russia were the main obstacles to global dominance, the United States described them as its primary enemies. China built up its military capacities and ordered nuclear weapons to overcome severe weakness in that department. Unless the United States acted before the delivery of those weapons, it seemed that China would be its equal. Washington acted most visibly by making Taiwan an American protectorate. To avoid nuclear annihilation, China acquiesced, and we may assume that the nuclear weapons order has been cancelled. Along with denying China access to the advanced chips made in Taiwan, it has used sanctions to deter China from competing in the most advanced fields of technology. It may succeed in preventing China for some time from competing with the United States in some types of advanced technology and weaponry.

Russia is fighting in Ukraine to maintain its position as a global power. When the USSR allowed Germany to be reunited, it was assured that the Western European countries, which had organized NATO to deter Soviet aggression, would not push forward against them. But when Russia gave up its empire and its Communism and hoped to be accepted, it was not. It was still the enemy, and NATO pushed forward close to the Russian heartland. Russia allowed this but repeatedly stated that it could not allow Ukraine to become part of a military alliance against it. It understood that NATO bases so close to its heartland would end its real independence. For some time, Ukraine elected presidents favorable to Russia and peace was maintained.

In 2014, the United States engaged in regime change against one of these presidents by stirring up nationalist Ukrainian feeling against both Russian Ukrainians and Russians. The new government broke its promise to give autonomy to the Russian Ukrainians, and areas dominated by these revolted. Ukraine sought membership in NATO. Russia had sympathized with the rebels, but it had done little for them. But when its survival as a world power was at stake, it invaded Ukraine and occupied ethnic Russian regions. Ukraine negotiated peace; but the United States blocked it. Boris Johnson, prime minister of Great Britain, flew to Kiev to assure the Ukrainians that NATO would do what was necessary to defeat Russia. Ukraine ended all negotiations.

Russia is a poor country, and originally the United States thought that extreme economic sanctions combined with the cost of war would bring Russia to its knees. This did not work. Western Europe suffered more than Russia from the sanctions. Destruction of Russian power would have to be through military means. The war continued to be fought in Ukraine, but the troops are trained and equipped by NATO. NATO's involvement will be whatever it takes to defeat Russia. Earlier care was taken not to provoke Russia into use of its nuclear weapons. But now it seems even that possibility will be considered. Victory will be the determinative success of the American goal. So close to success, the United States is unlikely to accept any compromise.

In alliance with China, it seemed that Russia might have succeeded. Now that China has yielded to American hegemony, the destruction of Russian power has become the top goal of NATO, and the war against Russia is NATO's war. Russia may yet win some victories, but it has little chance to compete successfully for global power. As we look and plan ahead, our task will be to operate in a world dominated by the United States alone. Our goal must be to persuade the United States to give priority to a habitable planet rather than to a global market. That is not a promising prospect.

First, military actions will continue. There are many countries in the Middle East, in Africa, and in Latin America that will try to reject American dominance. American dominance in the Western Hemisphere did not mean that Latin America was peaceful. American armies were repeatedly putting down those who struggled for independence. There is no reason to expect the global dominance of the United States to be peacefully accepted by all.

Second, the reason for the United States seeking unipolar dominance has been to create a single global market. Fighting of any kind makes that difficult. It is disrupted even by protests and strikes. As workers are further exploited and middle-class incomes fall behind inflation, social unrest will increase. The policies that make a single market "efficient" are just those that generate the most resistance and unrest from workers.

Third, no doubt technology will be used to slow the collapse of ecologies, the poisoning of the land, the rising of ocean levels, and other environmental disasters. But the ideology of the unified market cuts directly against the policies needed for human survival. Supporting industrial agriculture calls for insecticides. Without this, huge agricultural corporations would collapse. But the insecticides are exterminating pollinators. That will reduce the food supply massively. Who will win in Washington?

Fourth, as both nature and society become more chaotic, those who can live on local resources have the best chance of surviving. Our goal as environmentalists and humanists is sustainable local economies. This is the exact opposite of the ideology that is winning the global sweepstakes. At some point, of course, even Washington will understand this, but it is already very late.

12

What Should American Christians Do?
1. Learn the Truth

Fɪʀsт, we should inform ourselves about what our country has done and is doing in relation to other countries. With regard to current affairs, our rulers prefer that we remain ignorant and that we take no interest in them except on occasions when they want popular support for their actions. They prefer that we trust them to serve our national interest and that we retain the general assumption that the United States promotes democracy, human rights, and peace. As long as we are uninformed, we cannot be seriously critical.

The great majority of us Americans have accepted a situation in which we feel the importance of the victories of our favorite professional football team much more than the suffering of the people of Honduras under a military dictatorship we installed there. Indeed, we may not have noticed what we did there when it happened, and even if we did, we have forgotten. When thousands of Hondurans seek to enter the United States because their lives at home are threatened, we feel no responsibility for having created the conditions that drive them from their homes. The media make no connections; so, for us, there are none.

The silence of the media on most foreign affairs, and our collective indifference as Americans, feed on each other. The media thrive by publishing what people want to read; so, they keep us well informed about sports. We are affected in our judgment of what is important by what the media do and don't provide. Sports seem more important than international relations.

However, this does not entirely explain our collective ignorance and indifference. When they wish, the media can draw enormous attention to what is happening in other countries. Tens of millions of Americans, who would not have been able to locate Ukraine on a map, quite abruptly became deeply sympathetic with the people of Ukraine when the media told them Ukrainians were being attacked mercilessly and without provocation by the brutal Russians. The media told us this was important. Partly explicitly, and partly by repeated headlines, they persuaded us that the Russians are vicious and that we should punish them. Collectively, we believe what we are told to believe. The question of truth rarely arises.

In this situation, what should Christians do? They should seek truth and inform their fellow citizens. In the United States, the officially "free" press belongs to people for whom truth is not a major concern. They are part of the controlling group. Eisenhower called it the military-industrial complex and warned us about it. Today, Wall Street plays a large role. Some believe that global power still resides in the City of London.

The CIA is a major participant. It has its employees in every major newspaper company. Its members include elected officials and bureaucrats. Obama was a member of the CIA. It serves money far more than God. The foreign policy it advocates has been promoted by the neoconservatives building on their accomplishments on September 11, 2001.

Since the media, including *The New York Times,* are not primarily concerned about truth, the quest for truth pushes us elsewhere. We would rejoice if the churches had publications that cared about the truth. Sad to say, they do not. Nevertheless, there are places where we can find information that has not been filtered through concerns for acceptability or "political correctness." It would be good if some Christians worked together to locate and promote sources that could be trusted for information on what is happening globally. To supplement them, we could also check out sources that promote diverse points of view, so that we are helped to view events in various contexts. Perhaps some churches would decide their mission was to promote truth rather than political correctness.

If a group of Christians genuinely committed to truth decided to help their Christian friends to understand what is going on, there would often be disagreements among them. That would not make their work worthless. On the contrary, Christians also may see the world in diverse perspectives that highlight different aspects of what is happening. If members of the group are authentically Christian, they will know that their diverse perspectives are not the only ones, that only God's perspective provides the Truth. Reporting disagreements among Christians equally committed to truth and analyzing the reasons for them would be a truly valuable contribution. The project I am proposing differs from anything that now exists, but it can build on much that does exist. It lies "at hand."

Second, we need to learn how to distinguish between propaganda and reporting on the facts. This may be considered to be simply a part of getting accurate information. It is. But intentional and managed propaganda has its own character and calls for distinctive treatment.

In the first section of this chapter, I talked chiefly about the paucity of information and the importance of finding good sources. The problems with propaganda are different. It is not hard to find. It is everywhere. The problem is that it is easy to think that it is telling the truth and to be sucked into the story it tells.

For example, what has happened in Ukraine and why it happened is complex, but most of what we read treats it quite simplistically. This, by itself, warns us that we are reading propaganda. If we care to inform ourselves, the contrast between what is happening and how it is reported will illustrate in detail how propaganda works.

I described the situation in Ukraine in the previous chapter. Even my brief discussion showed something of the complexity in its contrast with the simple account with which the press bombarded us. We were told that, without provocation, Russia invaded an innocent neighbor and committed atrocities there. We are made to feel that we should do all we can against Russia and to help Ukraine.

It is important that those Christians who seek truth recognize that this is propaganda. This does not mean necessarily that the message is false. It means that those in charge want us to think about this topic rather than other equally important ones. And they want us to think about it in this way, quickly and contemptuously rejecting any other account.

There are many, many examples. For several days headlines dealt with a shell exploding in a train station in daylight hours. The headlines assumed that it was a Russian attack. Since we knew that disruption of communications had been a Russian priority, this was readily believable. But in a war, the shelling of a train station is not major news. What the headlines emphasized was that many civilians were killed. The message was that the Russians had committed another atrocity. Of course, this is propaganda, but most Americans, including Christian Americans, were hardened by it in their image of Russia as a cruel committer of atrocities. The propaganda was successful.

Only those who paid close attention had doubts about its truthfulness. They noticed that the Russians had shelled many train stations so as to disrupt the movement of Ukrainian soldiers, and the efforts to supply them with arms and food. However, in all other cases, Russian attacks on train stations had been at night, so that few people are killed. Why would they change tactics here when they could so easily wait until night?

There is also the question of what their purpose was in this attack. They had already found other means of disrupting the traffic they opposed. This attack on the station seems to have been a waste of their resources. Why engage in an action that would inevitably bring moral charges against them when nothing was to be gained?

Reflections like these do not prove that the propaganda is false. Those whose understanding had been shaped by propaganda did not know that Russia had tried to minimize civilian casualties. Even those who knew better did not thereby know that the current propaganda was false. So far as we knew, the propaganda might be true. However, the chances diminished when we learned the shell that killed so many civilians was the kind used by Ukraine.

What we should avoid is assuming propaganda in the guise of news is true just because we are told it is. We should keep open minds while asking for more evidence. One good question is: Who benefits? Current Ukrainian policy is to highlight Russian atrocities in order to maximize global public support. This fits that pattern. Russians lose. Ukrainians gain.

Another lesson we learned from Eisenhower is relevant at this time. Our media, less tightly controlled in those days, reported that the Soviets announced they had shot down an American spy plane. Eisenhower went on television to assure the American people that we had no spy planes. Evidence accumulated that the Soviet story was true. Eisenhower went back on TV to acknowledge he had lied.

What we learned, first, is that the president's job is to tell the American people what those who control the government thought it best we think. The president's job is to serve the interests of the nation. Truth is not a major factor in deciding what to say. Whether what he says is true is not of primary importance.

The point is not that considerations of this sort enable us to know what really happened. They do not. The point is that, if we reflect, we can be sure that what is presented as fact may not be so.

Another instance of American propaganda also deserves critical reflection. We were told that the Russians made a target of a Ukrainian lying-in hospital in Mariupol. A Ukrainian woman who was giving birth at that hospital at the time Russians were reportingly shelling it has announced that the story is false. She also reported that the hospital is a major center for the defending soldiers. Of course, this does not prove that the story is false. But, surely, we should not assume that the Ukrainian woman is lying. Perhaps, as she implies, the propaganda is fiction.

That Ukrainian soldiers occupy the hospital has been confirmed by others. If the Russians did shell those soldiers, the event still does not fit the description of a terrible atrocity. The unhesitating anger directed at the Russians that the story aroused in millions of readers was misplaced. We should learn to wait for confirmation before believing what each side in warfare tells about the other. We should find some way to get information about the probability of the truth of the propaganda to the people who again and again are inflamed by it.

We have reason to think that, like most people at war, Ukrainians tell lies when that has a chance of strengthening their cause. Most nations, including the United States, also engage in "false flag" operations. That is, they do terrible things that they can blame on their opponents. Almost certainly the destruction of three skyscrapers in New York on Sept. 11, 2001, was a false flag operation.

One may locate the explanation of the Russian invasion of Ukraine in various histories.

There is the history of the Ukrainian people who have suffered repeatedly at the hands of their much larger neighbor. One may locate it in the context of the Russian experience of betrayal of promises made by the West. I locate it primarily in the context of the American foreign policy goal of implementing unipolar dominance of a single world market. Americans have been taught to abstract the war from any context at all, holding that it was "unprovoked." The implication that Russia acted for no reason at all is a dead giveaway that we are dealing with propaganda. I have dared to hope that more thoughtful and generally better-informed Americans knew enough of the history to escape being caught up into this propaganda.

However, this morning, September 3, 2022, I received the summer issue of the *Bulletin* of the American Academy of Arts and Sciences. I was delighted to see that this issue, unlike most in the past, is devoted to a very important real-world problem: global instability and nuclear arms control. This bastion of academic norms is awakening to the responsibility to improve the understanding of current issues. But I was also disappointed.

The issue begins with an introduction to the problem by the president, David Oxtoby, whom I have long respected. At the top of the first page, in very large print, is a sentence that begins: "Russia's unprovoked invasion." This is lifted out of Oxtoby's article and seems to have caused no discussion within the Academy. If our finest scholars swallow this absurdity uncritically, it is difficult for me to hope for useful guidance from them. Such guidance must grow out of an understanding of the real situation. The American foreign policy goal of American domination of the world is of fundamental importance. If our best scholars put all the blame for conflict on those countries that have sought to maintain their independence, they will only contribute to the worsening of the situation.

I also received a request for funds from Peace Action. I believe the leaders of this organization are genuinely trying to persuade our government to support negotiations with Russia. Thus far the

U.S. has worked against negotiations so that the war would continue and drain Russia's resources. I wish them success. But their letter is aligned with America propaganda: Russia bad, Ukraine good: "Russia's illegal war of aggression" and "Russia's cruel invasion" alongside the "inspiring bravery" of the Ukrainian people. Negotiations with Russia by people who see Russians as vicious and Ukrainians as heroic victims is severely handicapped. It might be said that Russian-speaking citizens of Donbass have been heroically defending rights given them by an international treaty with the Ukrainian government which was then revoked one-sidedly by the government. Perhaps 15,000 have given their lives in this civil war. For them, Russians are liberators. Seeking peace while demonizing one side is shortsighted.

Propaganda also aims to determine our judgments of importance. While supposed Russian atrocities do matter, there are other things happening in the world that are of at least comparable importance but are barely mentioned. One day, while the main headline in my paper dealt with the train station, there was also a short piece about the fact that a million children are threatened with starvation in Afghanistan.

What is remarkable is that this story appeared at all. I admire the paper for publishing it. But we are led to think that fifty deaths caused by Russians in Ukraine is far more important than the deaths of hundreds of thousands of Afghan children caused by the U.S. refusal to allow the Afghans access to their reserves in American banks.

Why this disproportion? Perhaps because if the United States gave the current government of Afghanistan access to the reserves deposited by Afghanistan in American banks, the lives of these children might be saved. We have decided that it is more important to punish the rulers for having driven us out of Afghanistan than to save the lives of the children.

But if, day after day, the newspapers showed us pictures of

starving Afghan children, we Americans would not so placidly support our government's decision to let them starve. So, it is better to keep us focused on fifty lives lost in a railway station in Ukraine to fuel hatred of Russia than to inform us about Afghanistan. I hope that more American Christians will use common sense in the evaluation of American propaganda. (Subsequently the United States has announced that it will give half of Afghanistan's money to a humanitarian organization to feed the children. Incidentally, Biden has announced that the other half will be given to relatives of those Americans who died in 9/11. The Afghans who had nothing to do with 9/11 apparently have no right to influence how their money is used.)

13

What Should American
Christians Do?
2. Challenge the Goal

I HAVE made it clear again and again that there can be no real
peace and cooperation among nations as long as American foreign policy is devoted to unilateral domination of the planet by
one country, namely, the United States. Rejecting this goal is step
No. 1. I will begin this chapter with an expanded explanation of
why our opponents consider U.S. global domination to be the right
goal. Especially in a manuscript that begins with Jesus' call for us
to love our enemies, it will not do simply to talk about how to
defeat them. We must understand that at least some of our enemies
believe strongly that theirs is the right goal and that its pursuit
justifies the suffering that is involved in achieving it.

We are living in a time when money matters most to most
people. Let's consider ourselves. Practically speaking, what do we
want most for our children and grandchildren? Our decisions about

how to help them often suggest that we want them to have economic security. Perhaps that is not your highest priority, but it is probably high on your list. It is high on mine.

We are not concerned only for ourselves and our descendants. We would like for lots of people to have economic security, ultimately everyone. We know a reason for the economic security of so many Americans is because there is lots of money in circulation here. Overall, we know that, in general, countries where there is plenty of money give more of their people economic security. So, if we really want everyone to have economic security, we want all peoples to participate in an economically rich global system.

This system will produce goods and services as efficiently as possible. This efficiency is achieved by concentrating production where it is cheapest and distributing the goods as inexpensively as possible. The greater the freedom of corporations to produce and distribute, the more the world profits from the efficiency of the system.

Now, let us agree that some restrictions are needed. Poisons and radiation must be carefully managed. The health of workers must be safeguarded. The disposition of waste is important for everyone. Corporations must be checked by government. In the past, national governments have set standards for doing business within nations.

But now, increasingly, business is transnational. This makes it possible for more of us to have more things inexpensively. But because each country has its own rules, doing business across national lines is inherently complex and inefficient. Today we know that we must reduce the use of fossil fuels, but rules in different places are different, and everywhere they change frequently. Also, governments control fossil fuels, and trade in general, for political purposes. As a result, much of the benefit of a global system is lost. There is unnecessary economic insecurity for millions of people.

This could be changed if one government made one set of rules applied equally to all. Businesses would learn how best to work within a system and compete with one another in the quality and price of their products. With such competition, quality improves, prices are lowered.

We have sought to achieve a rational system through international cooperation in the League of Nations and the United Nations. We have achieved some local advances through trade agreements. The European Economic Community has vastly simplified business within Europe. But as long as most nations manage trade and investment for their own political gain, there will be great waste and uncertainty. Economic security will be limited to the few. It may be associated more with corruption than with good business.

What can be done? The transnational corporations need a unipolar world, that is, a world in which one nation sets the rules for all. That nation must understand and appreciate the needs of the corporations and enforce standardized practices. After World War II, the United States emerged clearly as the world's greatest power. It could have established a rule-based world and enforced the necessary order. But Americans had no coherent goal. Some enjoyed power and exploited those it dominated. Others were genuinely committed to the spread of democracy and human rights and hoped for a world of many democracies. Still others thought we should primarily manage our own affairs and leave the rest of the world to deal with theirs.

Still, there were some who saw the global responsibility of the United States and worked consistently for its implementation. The possibility for American unipolar dominance was slipping away, but it was not gone. What was needed was an incident like Pearl Harbor that would unite the people for global action. "A new Pearl Harbor" was arranged on September 11, 2001. Those who wanted the United States to govern the world quickly persuaded Americans to devote their energies to increasing its power and using it for the needed unipolar domination.

For centuries, the United States has dominated the Western Hemisphere. Europe has gone along with the post 9/11 program and accepted the domination of the United States. So have Israel, Australia, New Zealand, Japan, South Korea, and a number of other countries. Only two have clearly rejected the role they are asked to play and have the power to strongly resist: Russia and China. If they fall in line, resistance elsewhere will collapse.

For some years, Russia was the No. 1 enemy. It had an empire called the Soviet Union. American policy first successfully sought the collapse of that empire. Under Yeltsin, Russia seemed to be yielding to American global dominance, but Putin has made clear that Russia intends to defend its independence. The United States responded by opening the door of NATO to Ukraine. If Russia had allowed that, the United States could have controlled it. Only China would have remained. It could have been subdued.

I hope that I have exemplified the understanding of my enemies for which Jesus calls. Some of their leaders are idealists who may have made personal sacrifices and risked much for the sake of creating the better world they saw was possible. I hope that those who agree with me that this is the wrong goal will understand how thoughtful, well-meaning people can enthusiastically support it. Our task is not to demonize them but to show where they are mistaken. Of course, in this day when our schools teach the quest for personal wealth, selfish motives are also in evidence, but self-interest plays a role with most of us. Our task is to critique the ideas that lead to support of the wrong goal.

We can begin with basic priorities. This foreign policy assumes that the increase of global wealth is the top priority. We have known for half a century that we are already using resources faster than they can be replaced. Sustainability should have higher priority than growth. Those who give growth priority can make some concessions to sustainability. But thus far such concessions have fallen far short of what is needed. Instead, we should aim first for sustainability and then see what kinds of growth are still possible.

This is the first and sufficient reason for changing the goal of American foreign policy. However, there are other points of significant disagreement. It is assumed that once the United States took control of global affairs, its rule would be recognized as fundamentally just and for the sake of all. This is based on the assumption of "American exceptionalism." Our dominance of the Western Hemisphere for many years did not earn us this regard. We have forced acceptance with money and guns. Desire for freedom from our rule has increased rather than faded. My anticipation is that in Asia and in Africa, opposition to our domination would continue and grow. I believe that a quite different, bottom-up world order would do more to reduce wasteful warfare than a monopolar, top-down world order.

The supporters of the present order think that lying and killing are a small price to pay to establish what they want. I, on the contrary, think that any order built on war and lies is fundamentally unstable. There was a time when the American experiment in democracy captured the attention and imagination of people all over the world. The idea of being ruled by us would not have been offensive to many of them. But now that we have beaten so many into submission, we have lost that aura. We are feared more than we are loved. I do not believe that fear alone can be the basis of a global order over a long period of time.

My fundamental goal calls for the top priority to be sustainability. Of course, there would be many ways of seeking sustainability that would backfire. Any attempt to enforce all the needed changes with whips and guns would speed the self-destruction of civilization. Some of us have spent a lot of time thinking about the kind of society that we would find attractive and that would lure us into it.

We have chosen the name "ecological civilization" and a chapter has been devoted to it. All the other chapters are relevant. In an ecological civilization, people would love each other, including their opponents. They would put the wellbeing of the whole above their personal possessions. They would understand that although money is important to the functioning of society, human relations take priority. Truth would be highly prized. Special concern would be directed to those who are least considered. We would experience our kinship to other animals and our niche in the ecological system.

Of course, much of this will always remain aspirational. But we can seek to make ourselves a part of an ecological system that exists in partial ways here and there. It cannot be achieved by getting the U.S. government to announce that its goal is now an ecological civilization, although that would be a great advance.

What could happen in the political world? We could announce that in order to respond to current and impending threats, the United States will cease to seek power over others and will instead seek their cooperation in working for a living Earth.

In April of 2022 Ukraine and Russia negotiated peace. This is inherently a move from competition to cooperation. It could have saved many lives and much property and provided a basis for rebuilding Ukraine. However, since the goal of the United States was to destroy Russia as an independent power, this would definitely not help. The United States sent the prime minister of England to Kiev to persuade Ukraine to continue the war. Greater participation by NATO and greater generosity with ultra-modern weapons on our part followed, so that Ukrainians have killed a lot more Russians. The cost in Ukrainian lives has been high, but Ukrainians are strong nationalists. Unlike Russians and Americans, they are ready to give their lives for their country.

Surely it would not have been impossible to have allowed the peace agreement to go forward. A step in the direction of cooperation would have been taken. Surely such a step was "at hand." Asking our government to favor cooperation rather than forcing the subordination of all has immediate meaning and potential.

Around the time of the Glasgow conference (2021), an effort
to deal with climate change internationally, I thought there might
be an opportunity to shift American priorities. Mainland China
was our enemy after it drove Chiang Kai-shek's government to
Taiwan. For some years the world continued to view Chiang as
the true ruler of China. Finally, Nixon shifted American policy to
recognize that he was no longer head of state. Relations between
China, recognizing that the Beijing government was in principle
the government of Taiwan as well, were generally positive.

However, China's economic success and growing influence in
the Third World made it appear more of a challenge than a sec-
ondary participant. If the U.S. were to dominate the planet, China
must be held back. Obama pivoted to Asia, which meant that
limiting China had taken top priority. Biden repeatedly asserted
that China was America's No. 1 enemy.

Biden separated his concern to respond to global warming and
his commitment to the goal of universal dominance. For the latter
he built up an alliance of Asian countries against China. For the
former he asked for President Xi's cooperation. There had been
some cooperation on this all along, But Biden's actions against
China, combined with his rhetoric of enmity, was pushing Xi away.
It seemed likely he would not take part in Glasgow.

I thought it just possible that Biden might care enough about
the survival of civilization that he would place priority on that
rather than on weakening China. I thought any gesture in that
direction might help to shift priorities. I wrote a letter to the
two presidents asking Biden to stop calling China enemy No. 1.
I pointed out that China could not cooperate on climate in that
role. I asked Xi to recognize that any step toward friendship, however minor, might be costly to Biden politically, and that I hoped
he would respond with full cooperation on the climate. To my
surprise, Biden did publicly withdraw the label of "enemy" in
favor of "competitor," and Xi did go to Glasgow. Also, a new

committee, consisting of high-ranking people, was appointed by the two countries.

It seemed that if the new committee could seize the opportunity and take the global lead, the enmity of the United States to China might be subordinated to the saving of civilization. A fantasy? I suppose. But not an impossibility. Genuine cooperation to give us a chance for a living Earth was "at hand." The United States did not have to put enmity first.

Even if the United States had put cooperation with China ahead of enmity, and even if it had allowed peace to break out in Ukraine, American policy would not have become ideal. But once it recognized that dominating the world may not always be more important than peace and the survival of civilization, there would be a chance that the need to dominate might be subordinated to the need for a living Earth. It could happen. It is still "at hand."

Persuading the United States to adjust to a multipolar world order would be an enormous accomplishment. But it would still not be an ecological civilization. We should not forget our goal of a bottom-up world. In the destruction and chaos that are likely in our future, order on a large scale like the United States may collapse. Survival may depend on local economies and polities. If many people have clarity about what is possible, the idea of communities of communities might have traction.

A community-of-communities model of political organization was introduced in the chapter on ecological civilization. I believe it is also "at hand." The diminishing prospects for a survivable planet will force some consideration of change. Producing at a great distance from consuming will become more and more problematic. Supply lines will be damaged by storms and the social order required to maintain the current global system will decay. Even minor problems caused by Covid led to significant problems in moving goods. Much worse problems lie ahead.

The idea of local water supply, local food production, and local generation of energy is already part of the conversation. Pressure to use less gasoline will encourage less long-distance commuting as well as shipping. The idea of renewing old-fashioned communities has other attractions. Allowing these communities to have as much voice as possible in their own affairs is already considered as a respectable political position. Political self-government can develop as economic self-sufficiency increases.

Should there develop a number of nearby settlements, it will be almost certain that all will agree that they need to work together on common problems. Self-sufficiency in a group of villages can be more satisfying than in just one. Specialization in food production among them can also be helpful. So, a community of local communities is a very natural development.

My suggestion is that each local community select a couple of people to meet with representatives of other local communities. If there is great difference in size among the communities, some can have more representatives. Often these meetings will make proposals to be taken back to the local groups, but as time passes, they will take more actions on their own. If the local groups don't like what their representatives are doing, they can replace them at any time.

Obviously, the size of groups at each level may vary greatly. I'll offer figures just to suggest one possibility. Let's suppose that local communities have around two hundred adult members. Let's suppose that about twenty of them constitute the community of communities. The community of communities would have about four thousand adult members. The group that votes for the leadership of the next level will have forty or fifty members.

At the next level and at all above, I am concerned that the problems with money may arise. My proposal for reducing that is to avoid popular voting. At the local level, people will know those they vote for. Money will play very little role. But when it is time to select people to represent the community of local communities, the voters in the local communities will not know most of the candidates. Successful candidates are often the ones who have more money for self-promotion.

My suggestion is that the group of forty or fifty people elected to represent the local communities choose a couple of members of their group to represent the community of communities at the next level, the community of communities of communities. If this consists of twenty communities of communities, it will also have forty or fifty people representing around 80,000. If the 80,000 people voted, money would be needed to advertise the candidates, but with forty or fifty people voting, money should play a trivial role.

Obviously, the relation of citizens of local communities to those who make decisions at the level of a community of communities of communities of communities is impersonal. We are accustomed to think that allowing everyone to vote on these people is more democratic. My view is that limiting the candidates to someone who was initially selected by acquaintances and who has gained the respect of colleagues at several levels is more likely to put power in the hands of someone trustworthy and democratic in spirit. When people who have never been chosen by those who know them, but have spent a lot of money in creating an image, wins an office, I am not so confident. Since the expenditure of money has become so important, we often elect people who have a lot of money or who represent those with money. I believe the bottom-up structure I propose would greatly increase the prospects of the election of people who have demonstrated leadership qualities and concern for the people.

The overall plan may not be very different from that of some European countries. France was divided into sections that were divided into sections down, in some cases, to small villages that were economically largely self-sufficient. Usually the power was largely top-down, but there were partial exceptions. But until World War II, the inclusive community was the nation.

What happened in Europe at the end of World War II was the end of nationalism in the primary home of nationalism. France and Germany decided they would give up their sovereignty in order to end the primacy of competition among nations. Of course, there can be competition, but only in the context of community. Europe became the European Community. That is the model for countries elsewhere.

Sadly, it has not been followed. But this is not because of lack of interest. There have been efforts in both Africa and Latin America. Because the United States sees that continental communities of that kind would make it difficult to rule the world, its foreign policy has led it strongly to oppose these movements. Clearly, the possibility is "at hand." Letting things develop is not impossible.

My proposal would begin with Europe, add Latin America and Africa, and then recognize that there are two countries already larger than Europe: China and India. Adding them would give us five regions. Others are a bit more arbitrary. One might be a combination of Russia, Mongolia, and the "stans" including Pakistan and perhaps North Korea. Another might be the Near East, and still another Southeast Asia. The ninth could be the Anglo-Saxon world, plus such countries as Japan, South Korea, and Israel.

These regions have the advantage of the European experiment. My suggestion is that they not follow Europe into a single currency. The control of finances by the European Union has too greatly centralized power and diminished the self-determination of the nations. But decisions of this kind can be made in each case separately.

The really new experiment will be the community of these communities of nations. This will be another effort at a global organization with the power to maintain peace among its constituents. Hopefully, the very process of creating these regions and empowering them to do a lot for their people will shift the mindset from competition to cooperation. On matters of climate, for example, they will surely see that cooperation is needed with some power of enforcement located at the global level.

On many issues, decisions should be left to the continents and regions. Europeans and Americans should stop meddling in African affairs. Confronted by a united Latin America, the United States will surely recognize it is time to base relations on equality.

Our present foreign policy discourages cooperation and moves toward war. Is there any possibility of change? Perhaps we should also ask, if we do not change our foreign policy, does humanity still have a chance to survive? Perhaps we should accept the fact that our country is driving the human species to extinction and then ask, how can we survive anyway?

But for now, I ask, can we awaken the American people to demand that our nation commit itself to a living Earth rather than the most efficient and rapid economic growth? To hold as the ideal a system designed to speed up the collapse of the global ecology may be certified as "insane." Positive possibilities lie "at hand." Let's seize them.

14

The Gender of God
and the Role of Women
in the Church

CHRISTIAN HISTORY witnesses to the fact that God is as much female as male, or more. Of course, Jesus referred to God as "father," not "mother." But when we describe his "Abba," the tone is more feminine than masculine in terms of conventional distinctions.

Sadly, by the fourth century, the church had developed a doctrine of God based on the standard notions of masculinity rather than on Jesus' teaching. God was omnipotent, without feeling, demanding, absolute. As a result, when the church conquered the empire, the empire also conquered the church. The church that survived the collapse of the empire in the West was the Roman Catholic Church. Its headquarters were in Rome. Its language was Latin, the language of Rome. Its power structure and practice of leadership followed the lines of the Roman caesars much more than the Galilean Jesus.

Despite the masculinization and imperialization of the church, Jesus' Abba was not altogether lost. The gospels were still read, and the human Jesus was still admired. But the masculinization of Jesus as king of kings led to thinking of him more as people had long thought of God. And God could hardly be loved.

Increasingly, the feminine qualities of Abba were attributed instead to Mary, the mother of Jesus. It turned out that she could be turned into a divine being without losing those qualities. The young woman who bore Jesus, and about whom we know so little, became the Queen of Heaven and the Mother of God. And she was still experienced as deeply understanding the human situation and loving those who looked to her. The churches became places to worship her. God died, but his mother lived on. She functioned much as Abba had done in the early church in comforting the afflicted. She was not as strong on afflicting the comfortable.

The Protestant Reformation cut against this solution of the disappearance of Abba. There were glimmerings of recovery of the human Jesus and even of Jesus' Abba, but on the whole the Reformation moved in a patriarchal direction. On the other hand, variety was greater. There were more who redefined God as love and thereby recovered Abba in spite of the rejection of a female God. John and Charles Wesley understood the primacy of love and the movement they began was extraordinarily appealing to the common people.

The feminist movement has had a large impact. Few speak of God just as "she," but many acknowledge that using only male language is wrong. When pressed in any generation, most Christians acknowledged that God was neither male nor female. But feminists have made us aware of how badly our thinking has been distorted by exclusive use of male language. New thinking about God, truly free from masculine bias, has become genuinely possible. Perhaps we will understand the one whom Jesus called Abba better than did Jesus.

But there is another question about the very human women who have been members of Christian congregations. Until recently they have not been allowed to give leadership. Indeed, in many Christian cultures, wives have been virtual slaves of their husbands. Their role in church has been to silently serve the men. Christian men have been confused about what to do with their sexuality. For the mess they have made of this dimension of their lives, they blame the women. Going back to the Bible does not solve all of women's problems. Some it makes worse. Yet even through the stories told by men, it is clear that women played an important role among Jesus followers.

I am writing at Easter, 2022. We are told that the male disciples ran away when Jesus was being crucified. The women stayed with him to the end. The early Easter stories are all about the women disciples of Jesus. We get the impression from Mark that the men are moping around. The women are taking action. Matthew and Luke try to give the men some role, but it remains derivative. Take the men out of the Easter story; the story remains. Take the women out and there is no story.

The same is true of the birth stories in both Matthew and Luke. Take Joseph out; the story remains. Take Mary out; there is no story. Women are at the center of both Easter and Christmas. Take Easter and Christmas out of Christianity? Unthinkable.

Many Christians would agree that the Christianity of the persecuted church in the first few centuries was more deeply Christian than much of what ensued. Jesus was addressing oppressed people. When oppressors hear his message, they are not likely to understand it. They want to hear about God's power and glorious rule.

When the church allied itself with the Roman Empire, its most influential hearers were no longer the oppressed. The Roman Catholic Church in the medieval period spoke for the establishment, not for those oppressed by the establishment. Protestant churches that became state churches in northern Europe continued this tradition. Although Protestantism was not officially or politically established in the United States, in much of the country, it was culturally established. In the South, it was the religion of the slave owners; in the north, of the industrialists.

There was one church that was an exception. Despite what White Christians taught them, they heard the gospel as good news. Since they were not allowed to attend White churches, they had their own preachers and teachers. There were Black churches as self-governing parts of the larger Christian movement. Even before any of the ministers were allowed to read, they understood the Bible far more authentically than the White churches. They knew it spoke for their liberation. They understood their White oppressors far, far better than their oppressors knew them. They understood that mutual love among them was essential to their survival.

I will mention just one enormous, even astonishing, achievement of the Black Church, returning to the first chapter of the book. The Black preachers and teachers understood the importance of loving the enemy. Most of us would expect that the emotional effects of the cruelty to which they were subjected would be deep and abiding hatred, the hope that someday they could revenge themselves on their masters. Over the centuries that kind of hatred, given no opportunity for political expression, would have psychologically destroyed the slaves and their segregated descendants.

That did not happen. Black women were given the responsibility of childcare for millions of White children. The White children benefited greatly from their love. These women loved their enemies. Many a White woman employed a Black cook and housekeeper who also became a confidante. They loved the White women for whom they worked. That love went some distance, of course, not nearly far enough, to humanize some of the relationship between the races. Loving enemies is healing to the lover and touches a nerve in the loved oppressor. It was this deeply established teaching of the Black churches that made the success of Martin Luther King possible.

In some of the many nations colonized by European and American Christians, something similar has happened. The colonized people understand the gospel better than the colonial people who brought it to them. I have just learned that my tradition, Methodism, is spreading in the Philippines. I know, of course, that it is dying here. My guess is that the gospel we colonizers proclaimed falls far short of what some of the colonized heard. Jesus came through even when we did not know him.

Now we return to the main topic of the chapter: women. How might they save us in the White world who have reconciled our Christianity with imperialism, slavery, racism, capitalism, and the destruction of nature? We have, of course, also reconciled it with patriarchy, even with extreme forms that have virtually made wives the slaves of their husbands.

The problem of these women in dealing with their oppressors was even more intimate than that of slaves. They were expected to love those who often bullied and abused them. Even when these others were personally kind and loving, they almost inevitably exploited them. Indeed, part of their expected role was to make their husbands look good. That many women have been able genuinely to love their husbands in a relationship designed to exploit them is an impressive achievement. We can hope that some of them have been helped to love by their Christian faith.

Let us consider the role women have played in promoting the gospel even when they were treated as subordinates. We have already noticed that even though the gospels are written in an accepted patriarchal culture, they do recognize that women played an important role. When the male disciples fled, women surrounded Jesus on the cross. Women were the first to tell the still frightened men that Jesus had risen. It seems that from the beginning they understood Jesus better.

I am theorizing that they understood Jesus better because they understood oppression better. They were oppressed not only by Rome but by Jewish society. They may have understood better that responding to oppression with love is key.

Probably most of the gatherings of Christians in the first centuries were in homes. Even if the expected role of the women was to prepare and serve rather than to participate, their part was very important. The persecuted Christians were noticed by their love for one another, a love nurtured in these house churches. My guess is that the women actually led in this mutual love.

This mutual love expressed itself also in responding to the needs of the larger community. This played a large role in the rapid growth of the faith. My guess is that when it came to the actual feeding of the hungry and visiting the sick, the women played a very large role.

One possibility for the future of the gospel in the United States is that alongside of the bureaucratically operated, building-centered churches of the past, we return to house churches. This time, the role of women will not be limited to preparing and serving. These house churches can be very diverse. I attend one, Church of Our Common Home, led by a woman, Bonnie Tarwater, on a five-acre farm. It especially celebrates the human connections with the land and trees and the domestic animals. We understand that love is the key, and that the human future depends on a shift of the human relation to the rest of nature from exploitation to communication and love. We delight in worshipping with the goats and chickens.

In our worship we draw extensively from the work of women, but men are not excluded. Bonnie especially likes to draw on male/ female pairs: Jesus and Mary Magdalene; St. Francis and Sister Claire. She likes to think of the couple in terms of a welcoming female and a joyful male response. Sometimes she seeks an image of the divine in that kind of union of the female and the male principles. That might be better than Jesus' Abba as the object of worship.

I will continue this expression of hope first with a word of caution. Introducing women into leadership positions in the existing mainstream American churches is a good expression of commitment to end discrimination against women. However, its overall effect on church life and practice has been minimal. The male-dominated churches have ceased to have apparent importance. Simply changing the gender of their leadership will not change that.

Nevertheless, as we look at our recent histories, we will see that where women have shaped their own institutions within the church, the gospel is more effectively visible. In the Roman Catholic Church, the sisters have led in most of its best work.

I will conclude with my experience of the place of women in the Methodist church. The closest analogy to the Catholic sisters was the Women's Society of Christian Service. There were chapters in most churches, and they were more oriented to their regional and national leadership than to the leadership of the local church or the bishop. They had their own missionaries around the world. My parents were missionaries sent out by the church's Board of Missions. But I learned, growing up, that my parents were a bit jealous of the women missionaries. They and those who supported them were better organized and did a better job.

In local churches in Georgia, the church school was often the most important part of the church. We took up collections in both, but the schools had a certain autonomy. They were not officially part of the women's responsibility, but they were chiefly led and staffed by women. Teaching in a church school was a significant volunteer position. Teachers took classes to improve their teaching skills. They were often more acquainted with the best literature on education than the public-school teachers. Many of them did serious reading on the content of teaching as well. These Sunday morning classes were where children learned about the faith and its implications for life. Then, Sunday evening, youth gathered for their own programs, of course with adult guidance.

There were male teachers and administrators in the educational program, but in most churches, it was run by women. In many towns these Sunday Schools were the most important volunteer programs. They did much to shape the community. What I learned in Sunday School was responsible Christian teaching. I cannot recall any defense of segregation. Occasionally there were teachers strongly favoring integration.

As the prospects of forced integration became clear, I was invited by the Women's Society for Christian Service to give talks at each of the ten districts in North Georgia. I had several hundred women in each event. I spoke strongly in favor of integration and felt that the women largely agreed. I do remember that two walked out of one meeting. But the women's leadership had prepared this segment of middle-class White Georgia women to affirm integration as the way ahead.

I do not think anything comparable could be said about the men and will conclude with an amusing incident. When restaurants began to integrate, some leadership group of men announced that they would boycott integrated restaurants. The next day a leadership group of women announced that they would not. That was the last we heard of the boycott. I am hopeful for women's leadership.

A bit more concretely, we can expect that with the collapse of so much of what we have enjoyed, what survives will be local and small-scale. If others come to agree with me that Jesus is one whose life and teachings deserve our continuing attention, some may gather in homes to study and support one another. If Christianity survives at all, it may be in such house churches, similar to the ones in which the church began.

Although gender differences are lessening, I guess that women will on the whole turn out to be better at gathering these groups and nurturing mutual love among those who come. Perhaps some of them will understand Jesus well. Perhaps they will embody love of neighbors, including enemies, serving life and God rather than competing for wealth, Perhaps they will be genuinely open to truth wherever that leads thinking and action. Perhaps, together with other small groups, they can become the foundations of an ecological civilization.

15

Can Women Save
Discipleship to Jesus?

WRITTEN BY REV. BONNIE TARWATER

John Cobb has asked a good question. Can woman save Christian discipleship? My answer is yes. We are doing it already! Creative change often comes when the old ways are not working any more.

The Christian church, like so many institutions in the modern world, is falling apart during this planetary crisis. Currently the war in Ukraine has made nuclear annihilation of all life on Earth a grim possibility. The U.S. empire is spending trillions on the military for wars that are suicidal. The collapse of ecosystems and species and the ecological catastrophe are escalating far faster than anyone predicted. Personally and collectively, many of us are also falling apart. We are affected by our planetary situation no matter how hard we act as if we can separate ourselves from other creatures. There is hope, however, for every crisis is an invitation for growth, healing, and transformation.

If a church is not telling the truth about our planetary crisis, it is not relevant, in the same way that if Jesus had not told the truth about the Roman Empire, his teachings would not have been relevant for the people of his time. The Way of Jesus invites us to walk with him on two paths: one is the prophetic path of truth-telling, and the other is a mystical path. Humans will stay awake for the bad news of the world if we live connected to God's love in families and/or communities that support and love us. The mystical path honors our love affair and communion with God. Both prophets and mystics are needed now in loving partnership within us and amongst us.

As a recent convert to a God worldview and the teachings of Jesus, I tend to be extremely passionate about the Good News that God loves us, and there is nothing we can do about it. I long to talk about how God is working in my life and to pray with others. I want to tell the truth about how dangerous the world is now. It is hard for me to find people who want to do both. I feel lonely when I am with people in religious communities, in my family, and in my neighborhood, among people who are either in so much denial that they are not interested, or they are belligerently disinterested that we are living during the sixth extinction of life on Earth—the only one created by us humans. Why hasn't the church been telling the truth about this for the last seventy years? Why hasn't it offered us ways to respond more effectively? We are on a suicidal path as a human family, killing our own habitat, our common home, Mother Earth. She is sick, and it is past time for us to gather around her bedside and pray; to ask God for help, to ask God for healing, for her and all her creatures, all of whom are our family in the natural world.

John Cobb is one Christian who has been telling us the truth, and for a long time. His book, *Is It Too Late?* the first book-length philosophical and theological analysis of the environmental crisis, was published in 1971. He has been bravely countercultural in giving us a worldview that bridges physics and Alfred North Whitehead and God. He has supported many of us—his women students—in the same radical way as Jesus. Jesus supported women in the ancient world. Supporting women in the patriarchal institutional madness of the "Church" is as radical now as it was then. Men out there, women in religious leadership still need your support.

WOMEN IN THE CHURCH CARING FOR OUR MOTHER EARTH

The modern world is, in a word, lonely—lonely, lonely, lonely. Many of us do not have the loving family and communities we need and want. Women in the church can and must show leadership by responding to our modern epidemic of loneliness with welcome, hospitality, and radical love. We want to lift up, model, and support intimate personal relationships as sacred and at the center of the teachings of Jesus.

I thank all of you who are providing loving community in churches and other faith communities, for you do God's work in our lonely modern culture. I love my church and find great meaning in being with people and our beloved animals and plants in the barn every Sunday, as we study the teachings of Jesus, pray to God, sing and dance as well as learn about what is happening in the world and explore how we can be of service. We share the News of Hope and Vision as we share our Twelve-Step Program for Ecological Civilization.

We are called to make a loving welcome and place at God's table for the least of these, and today it is the creatures in the natural world who need to join us. Perhaps it will be women who have the common sense and decency to invite them in. Women have made many contributions to a more loving and inclusive church with creative rituals and new liturgies, and gender-inclusive language for God. Some of us have celebrated children, shared more personally in pulpits, and supported intergenerational family life as the heart of community. Now we need to widen the circle to creatures in the natural world. We need them to be included in our families, churches, and in our community work. It is the plants, animals, and ecosystems that have been left out of the church, and we women are called by God to show leadership, to create sacred circles with all creatures included and cherished.

Hildegarde of Bingen, from the eleventh century, was a mystic who had visions and who, with the support and encouragement of a loving male colleague, was able to write about her mystical experiences in later life. She taught us that angels travel faster than thoughts. Hildegard, the artist, musician, theologian, healer, writer, teacher, and creator of female monasteries, was a visionary who had great influence in the wider world, including on popes and princes. She calls us as women both to claim our mystical experiences and to reach out to effect change in our world. Both are urgently needed at this historic time We will not solve our problems using the same means we used to create them. It is time for us to claim our mystical traditions and move out into the world, not just to care for our families, but to provide religious leadership for our spiritual global crisis.

In 2015 my denial about the severity of our planet crisis broke open as I worked with John Cobb on his Seizing an Alternative ecology conference. With the support of a loving husband, we began a new house church. I felt God was calling me to dedicate my ministry and the rest of my life's work as a minister to the love and care for our common home Mother Earth in more radical ways than I could find in a more traditional church setting. We used Pope Francis' term "care for our common home" from *Laudato Si,* his 2015 encyclical, and named our church, dedicated to Mother Earth, Church for our Common Home. Like many women, I needed a break from serving in the patriarchal traditional church.

Many men and woman today have left the traditional church but long to explore and experiment with more relevant expressions, like new house churches that are exploring partnership models to love and care for all creatures. Women need the support of loving, supportive women and men, husbands, sons, teachers, and friends as we experiment in leadership positions.

Yes, many women are now ordained, but it is still extremely difficult to navigate patriarchy in the world and in the church. It has been for me. I know some loving men and some unloving women, and we know that patriarchal dominant-over models have formed and deformed us all in tragic ways. We all have been brainwashed and harmed by our dominant-over systems of injustice, whether they have been colonialism, White supremacy, patriarchy, or hierarchy in any form—you know, where one guy at the top tells everyone else "beneath" him what to do. Together, God calls us to explore how to dismantle patriarchy and create new partnership models for our families, the church, and all our communities.

John Cobb has eloquently shared the urgent need for transdisciplinary ways to understand the world. Patriarchy cannot be partitioned off as a separate issue, disconnected from environmental issues, economics, politics, and so on. We are invited to see and have visions of an ecological civilization with justice for all creatures as we live with holistic understandings of life.

John Cobb's ecology conference and Pope Francis' *Laudato Si* were both profound gifts to the world, "coincidentally" created in 2015 from two of our most important ecological Christian leaders. This was the year that my denial about the severity of our Earth crisis was broken open in a big way. Many of us are awakening to the cries of Mother Earth from deep inside her. We are interconnected with the divine feminine. She is calling us to share, write, and make artwork about our experiences as we invite others to share how God is working in our lives.

Our patriarchal religious traditions purposely have left women out, dishonored and abused them as well as the whole natural world, so yes, I understand why you may think traditional religions are hopeless. But instead of giving up on Christianity, let's just move out of the institutional patriarchal madness and take our worship and communities out into the natural world. Let's include and talk to the animals and trees and offer prayers for Mother Earth and all the creatures and ecosystems.

RE-INVENTING CHRISTIANITY

Are women creating a kind of new religion? John Cobb calls us to create a new religion he calls Earthism. Woman have already contributed to a new ecofeminist consciousness in recent decades with advances in process and ecofeminist theologies, feminist biblical scholarship, and such archeological finds as the Gnostic gospels of Mary and Thomas (discovered 1896 and 1945, respectively).

Women who love the teachings of Jesus are saving discipleship when we get radical and join with others around the world who find Jesus' teachings relevant. Some of us are reinventing and re-imagining Christianity, as we honor our common home, Mother Earth. This love of Earth as Earthists has changed the teachings of Jesus for many of us. God is inviting us to intertwine new images, symbols, and stories with our older stories and symbols to include the natural world too often left out of Christianity and the world religions. Some of us are experiencing a planetary consciousness-raising as we learn about the history of patriarchy and misogyny at the same time as we learn about the genocide of our planet. Something clicks within us, and we have an "aha" experience as we make these connections. What we have done to women's bodies we have done to our Mother Earth's body. It becomes deeply personal as we join in sisterhood with mothers and children of all species who love their families and are desperate to provide a future life for their loved ones.

Images of the Black Madonna have become a common symbol of this rich interwoven experience of God coming out of the Earth.

She is speaking to us. We are being called to be in intimate relationship with her, to listen to her, and to communicate with her.
Many of us have become mesmerized by the stories and artwork
about the Black Madonna. The Black Madonna, God, and the
Earth are suffering. All three have been dishonored by the patriarchal religions.

Artwork of the Black Madonna, coupled with photos of our
Earth taken from outer space, are my chosen religious icons relevant
for this time. Some astronauts experiencing this new perspective of
our common home from outer space called it a mystical experience,
a God experience. Like these space travelers, we are also in awe as
we gaze on the beauty of Mother Earth in these space photos and
in our imaginations. Some of us have also had a mystical God experience from just imaging what the astronauts actually experienced
with this new perspective from outer space. It is an experience of
our oneness and the interconnected web of life, where everything
every creature does here on Earth and in the cosmos affects every
other creature and ecosystem, every earth worm and galaxy. We
can now see with our eyes Mother Earth as a whole being. We can
feel with our hearts and spirits that she is our common home, our
Mother, a living organism with needs and feelings.

The photos of the Earth for me invite both the new organic
worldview that needs to change the way we think, but it also invites
us to fall in love. May our new love affair with our beloved Mother
become the mystical God experience modern people need to wake
us up, to change the way we live. Just like the astronauts, it is a
deeply meaningful journey for our human family to leave home
in order to come back home in awe and gratitude.

Catholic women greatly inspire me. Their struggles to stay in
a patriarchal church are a testament to their love for God and the
teachings of Jesus. As one Catholic woman shared, "They would not
ordain us women, so instead of taking care of everyone, we went
to the library and rewrote Christian theology." They have done

exactly that, beginning in the 1960s, gifting us with "A God we can do business with," as we say in twelve-step programs. Catholic women challenged the patriarchal theology that brainwashed so many into believing that God had supernatural powers and was like a punishing Father, King, Lord, Master, and separate from us. These women gave up on that God (who is not even biblical) and re-gifted us with the God who co-creates with us, the God who is more like Jesus' Abba God, who is more like a loving Mother, Sister, Friend, and Lover. Ecofeminist and process theologies have reconnected us to the natural world and laid out a new path, a Way, to retain the teachings of Jesus as we transform our religion into an Earthist religion that is relevant for modern people who are falling in loving with and caring for our Mother Earth. There is life after all the old stories that have been our steady diet for 2,000 years about a celibate son and his virgin mother.

PASSIONATE LOVE IN PARTNERSHIP WITH
OTHER CREATURES BECKONS US FORWARD

Inviting Mary Magdalene to stand in partnership with Jesus invites us to make the family the central story and relationship in a way that our stories about a celibate son and virgin Mother never could and never will be able to. In her groundbreaking book, *The Women with the Alabaster Jar,* Catholic laywoman Margaret Starbird—not a celibate nun but a wife and mother of five children—has written a revisionist story that introduces us to Mary Magdalene as the lost bride of Christianity. She helps make the teachings of Jesus thrilling and life-giving again. This book was a source used by Dan Brown to write *The DaVinci Code.* His blockbuster book and movie is a revisionist story that invigorated the religious imagination of millions around the world. Margaret Starbird and I both disagree with Dan Brown's choice of making the story about a bloodline, for this is the opposite of what Jesus taught. Clearly, Jesus taught us to love those we are not related to and to treat everyone as our family, not just our blood family.

Although Brown brought this nonbiblical focus to his book, he did us a great service by experimenting with new, more relevant stories about Jesus that include women. Cynthia Bourgeault's brilliant book, *The Meaning of Mary Magdalene,* further explores how the passionate love that Jesus and Mary Magdalene shared shines through history in legends and artwork, and resonates with our own personal experiences. She asks, where did Jesus learn this radical new love, even of enemies? Maybe Mary Magdalene taught Jesus about this passionate radical love! Well, maybe they taught one another. This is a much better story!

These new stories have ignited our religious imaginations as they bring back the lost bride, the Holy Grail, the Black Madonna, the one who was hidden and left out. No wonder King Arthur could not find the Holy Grail, chalice or cup, for they were looking in all the wrong places. The Holy Grail is a woman's womb inside her body. Biologists today share the remarkable truth that inside the womb, the egg is vastly larger than the sperm. The egg actually opens uniquely for a specific sperm. This feels significant—that we are all made in welcoming love. Many of us long to live in a partnership model with men and women and with the natural world, welcoming one another in tender and passionate love, and with a God who loves us all the way down to our shared cellular existence.

Jesus' teachings are about passionate love for our children, lovers, co-workers, friends, spouses, grandparents, neighbors, chickens, trees, daffodils, water, whales, galaxies, GOD....If you want to save someone—love them. As a rabbi once said, "The Bible is holy but the Song of Songs is the Holiest of the Holy." Passionate sexual love is what has been missing from our stories about a celibate son and virgin mother. We need to infuse our religion, our Christianity, the teachings of Jesus, with passionate love—love for our lovers, God, Mother Earth, and all God's creation.

There are many women today and in history who have found a way when there seemed to be no way. Leymah Gbwoee is a Nobel Peace Prize winner who inspired and led a successful nonviolent civil disobedience movement in Liberia that overthrew one of the worst genocidal modern dictators in recent history, Charles Taylor. How did she do this? Her movement began with her truth-telling about her own abuse, her service to other abused women, and her invitation to Christian and Islamic woman to gather together in prayer.

Women will save Christian discipleship when we make our church communities relevant to the real dangers in the world threatening all those we love. Women can share their prayer lives and closeness with God. We can also commune with women in history and invite communion with the saints, both those known to us and those unknown. According to Walter Wink, the earliest record of civil disobedience was in 500 BCE, when a group of midwives refused to do what Pharaoh commanded. They refused to kill babies. May we call upon our fearless ancestors, like the midwives from thousands of years ago, and lead acts of civil disobedience to protect children.

We need sensual and sexual women who celebrate their own animal natures and love of nature. Women are called to welcome the natural world, animals and plants, into our religious imagination and our worship. We need women who are able to channel their sexual passionate love energy, different at every stage of life, into meaningful work for our beautiful habitat for future generations.

Liberal Christianity and Catholics must show leadership today. We must come together to invite the ecumenical community and the world religions to our tables of warm passionate, welcome and hospitality, to eat, talk, pray, and work together, and to love one another deeply. Let's stop being prisoners to political correctness and fall in love. When people are in love, they are filled with energy, joy, playfulness, and creatively. They want to serve their beloveds in tenderness and care.

LIBERAL CHRISTIANITY VERSUS REAL PEOPLES' NEEDS

The idea for this book came about during meetings for the Living Earth Movement, John Cobb's latest organization with the mission to inspire global cooperation for the sake of all life on our planet, beginning with the United States and China. A small group of us who wanted to contribute something of value to a movement for a living Earth, not a dead one. After all, Mother Earth is a living organism, a creature with feelings. We were interested in many possible different ways to contribute positively. Some wanted to teach about ecological civilization, others were interested in second-tier diplomacy; still others wanted to work with political leaders or young people and citizen diplomacy. I was the only one who wanted to work with religious leaders and faith communities. Maybe it is because I did not grow up in the church, and, naively, I come with a zealous enthusiasm. I know you and I can agree on one thing. We know in our bone marrow that we need religious leadership now. We need to be God's hands and feet as we develop our prayer practices, provide music, rituals, old and new stories, loving faith communities that do social justice work, and teach a new worldview. Where can we find all this potentially in one place? In our religious traditions.

It is time for liberal Christians to claim the power of our prophetic tradition in partnership with the passionate love affair that is Christian mysticism. The human family has never experienced such an existential crisis, nor has our Mother Earth in her 4.5-billion years of life. It is past time to live more like a Mother Bear, who fearlessly saves her babies from predators, with passion, strength, and deep, instinctual, radical love.

SHARING OUR GOD EXPERIENCES

At the end of the wonderfully dark comedy, *Don't Look Up*, the characters have a last supper in the tradition of the early disciples who broke bread together every week in house churches. In the movie they have dinner and someone asks for something they don't usually do. Pray. Except she doesn't know how. Fortunately, one of them had gone to church and knew how. As they wait for their impending death from the fast-approaching, Earth-destroying comet, they all want to talk to God. Maybe seeing this movie would be a good way to begin conversation in a small group. We use the prayer from the movie at our church, Church for Our Common Home, but I changed the problematic masculine and all-powerful God language from, "Father and Almighty Creator" to something more inclusive.

God language has been one of the main reasons the church and all patriarchal religions have become irrelevant for many. It will take thousands of years to change how we have been formed and deformed by patriarchal religions, and we may not have that long. In the meantime, let's just change the hierarchal male language about God as one quick way to make the teachings of Jesus more inclusive. Not a God that is almighty, all powerful, or a punishing father-type God who looks like the God painted on the Sistine Chapel. For many of us, the teachings of Jesus become relevant if we just change the way we address God in prayer. Our hearts will follow. Here, I offer the prayer having changed God's name, but not the prayer.

> Dear Mother Father God, you whom we call by many names, we ask for your grace tonight despite our pride; your forgiveness despite our doubt. Most of all we ask for your love to see us through these dark times. May we face whatever is to come in your divine will with courage and open hearts of acceptance. Amen.

My husband and I recently purchased a small five-acre farm in Oregon. We have named it the John Cobb Eco Farm and are exploring biodynamic farming, created by Rudolph Steiner. Steiner is the father of organic farming, but he is not mentioned in universities or the academy. Why? Because he had mystical, visionary experiences, was telepathic, and was a profound spiritual teacher. Steiner was a genius who, like Alfred North Whitehead, rejected the Cartesian dualistic, materialistic worldview and offered his ideas of an organic world. Farmers came to him and shared their concerns that, although their ancestors had farmed the land for generations, something had gone very wrong. Something was wrong with the soil. He told them that the poisons in fertilizers and insecticides were killing it. Of course, indigenous peoples before Steiner did not use these poisons so they were doing what we now call "organic farming." Rudoph Steiner was the first person to name this problem in the modern era, and his solution he called biodynamic farming.

You don't have to be a genius to know that what Steiner taught is the truth. The poisons in agriculture are killing us. All you need is common sense to stop using poisons in the soil, for obviously it gets into our food and animals, which gets into our bodies and makes us all sick. Not only that, but our food also no longer provides the vitamins we need to live healthy vital lives. Steiner offered a metaphysic for agriculture, a God worldview. Our vision for Church for Our Common Home is to explore growing healthy food as we learn about biodynamic farming. The vision includes an organic worldview, prayer, and worship of God. We invite people of any faith or no faith to come love and be loved by the natural world. Nature is a universal place where many people in all faiths feel communion most strongly with God.

We have created an interfaith Secret Prayer Garden, with Twelve Tree Prayer Stations over five acres. Each Tree Station invites us to sit on the ground with our backs up against the tree and pray for the Earth. Our Living Rosary invites prayers for the soil, water, and animals at the John Cobb Eco Farm, and for all creatures on Earth. We honor many of the ancient world's religions and invite prayers to develop inner Fruits of the Spirit, including, love of enemies and forgiveness, generosity, gentleness, and so on.

There are, of course, many ways to pray, and some of us consider artmaking, dancing, cooking, lovemaking, dream-sharing, counseling, and being in the natural world all to be powerful ways of connecting to God.

I have led dream groups for many years and found dream-sharing to be an ancient spiritual practice whose time has come back. My calling to begin a house church began with a BIG dream in 2015. In my dream, a snake—a huge snake, red, white and black—filled an enormous community room, splashing in water that is above my knees. I am standing in the water. This giant snake bites my right hand and will not let go. I am calling out for help, calling to my son Ben. "What should I do? It hurts!" I hear the words as if from God, "Remember to breathe. It is like Lamaze." Lamaze is the practice many of us learn when we are pregnant and getting ready to give birth. Giving birth is painful. Waking up from denial to the truth of our global crisis has been a painful process. A huge force, abnormally huge and unlike anything I have ever encountered, has bitten me awake and commands me to engage in an ancient practice of breath work for pain and in readiness for a birth.

Anne Barring is a global leader and scholar in the study of the Divine Feminine who has little affection for Christiainty. In 2015, I read her wonderful book, *The Dream of the Cosmos, A Quest for the Soul*. I'll never forget one early morning when I first opened this book and read the dream that she says inspired the book. In Anne's dream a snake bites her on her right hand. She notes the play on words to 'write' or 'right' a book, and she believes this dream inspired her to write a book about a dreaming cosmos. That our dreams were so similar got my attention. Then, about the same time I had a snake dream and read Anne Barring's snake dream, I also heard a similar dream from a woman in my weekly dream group. An Islamic woman and organic farmer shared a dream about being bitten on her hand by a snake. This synchronistic God experience is something I don't fully understand but feel as a deeply meaningful coincidence.

Many of us have been taught how to think psychologically, but we have been so brainwashed by our secular culture and atheism that we don't know how to begin to develop a relationship with God and to honor our prayer lives. We do not need support groups based solely in psychological practices, for psychology has too often dehumanized people with clinical diagnoses and drugs. We need radical loving relationships, for love heals people. If women are going to help save Christian discipleship today, they will have to invite and model loving, welcoming relationships, and small communities with prayer and intentionally developing passionate love for God. I challenge you, the reader, to learn more about the abundant scientific research on how intercessory prayer works. Just because we don't yet know how it works scientifically does not mean it is not real.

DISCIPLESHIP AS A PARTNERSHIP MODEL WITH JESUS AND MARY MAGDALENE

Why do we need to write a revisionist story about Mary Magdalene? For many women who are working in the patriarchal religions we need to reconnect to our own ancestors like Mary Magdalene. Mother Mary guided me as a young single mother, and now as a minister working in the world with men, I need a loving woman as a role model to guide my ministry and work today. I want to work with other men like John Cobb and Pope Francis in partnership. I began going to a UU church because they had co-ministers, a husband and wife team, and when I was going through a painful divorce I would go to church and cry. Witnessing their religious partnership inspired me, in part, to go into the ministry.

The partnership of Jesus and Mary Magdalene that has been revealed with new historical evidence is empowering for us as women as we begin pioneering loving partnerships with men. I am inspired by Rev. Dr. William Barber and Rev. Dr. Elizabeth Theoharis who, in a gender and racial partnership, are doing inspired work with The Poor People's Campaign, calling America to a moral revival for our country. Well, it is past time we follow in their footsteps to offer religious leadership for a moral revival for our planet. It is past time we organize religious leaders and faith communities to work, men and women together. Religious organizations need to partner with secular organizations like Code Pink, which for over twenty years has been working for world peace. They have gone into the streets with civil disobedience actions against war and the insane, suicidal trillion-dollar military complex here in the USA. We need the equivalent movement in the church!

Christianity has become largely irrelevant for many modern people, not because of the teachings of Jesus, which many of us recognize as lifesaving and profoundly meaningful and desperately needed at this historic time. It is our stories *about* Jesus that need some rewrites. Modern people will not be able to stay with these teachings if we keep telling exclusively the story about Jesus, the celibate son, and his mother, a virgin. I do not want to stop telling these brilliant, beautiful, and deeply meaningful stories, but we can add new stories about the partnership of Jesus and Mary Magdalene. We can new stories about the partnership that we humans have with the natural world and all other animal and plants, so necessary now for our global crisis. They are similar stories, of course, just as the model of adult women and men in intimate physical and psycho-spiritual relationship shows how we need to become adult men and women in an intimate psycho-spiritual relationship with the natural world. The Good News is that this is a relationship filled with pleasure and passionate love and adventure. The Bad News (it may feel bad at first, but it will make us feel great, actually) is that we as humans have to grow up and mature if this partnership is really going to be loving and life-giving.

We do not have historical evidence either way to prove that Jesus was married or was celibate, but the story we have been telling for two thousand years about a celibate son and his virgin mother has lost its meaning for us. Religious stories are, of course, filled with symbolism and are not meant to be taken literally. As someone who was educated as a visual and performing artist and has worked as a drama and art teacher, I despair at the literal turn of our culture. The idolizing of the mind and the lack of arts education for our children has resulted in a major problem for modern people when it comes to celebrating symbolism. Virginity often is a symbol about purity and does not need to be taken literally. John Cobb has written in previous chapters about how added traditions and bad translations of the Bible have too often become the dogma and teaching of the church. Frequently this is far from anything remotely relevant to what Jesus actually taught.

Why not honor the traditional stories *and* be open to new revisionist stories about Jesus as well? I want to celebrate the deep symbolic meaning of the virginity of Mother Mary, for example, which expresses the goodness and purity of the mother-baby relationship. I was profoundly nourished myself, as a young girl, by the deep meaning of the story of Christmas, with the nativity set I played with on our coffee table, and I did not even go to church! Our patriarchal world must make the connection between the dishonoring of young girls, the divine feminine, and Mother Earth herself—we share a similar wound. Our Christian story beautifully expresses the real purity that is every young girl, a new young creature. We must honor these sacred stories. A young girl gives birth surrounded by peaceful animals in a stable. Let's keep this powerful story that invites us to reconnect to our miraculous animal nature and with God. We can invite revisionist stories, like they did in the early church.

Many of our cherished stories differ one from the other in the New Testament. For example, the different gospels tell different Christmas stories. We conflate these accounts in our imaginations and believe they are one big story. The gospels were not journalistic stories relaying facts; rather they are invitations to bless us with deep meaning. They were first an oral tradition, and they are not even original! There are many other examples of virgin birth stories, as well as stories similar to our Easter story.

The Easter story was inspired by stories that came out of goddess cults and pre-Christianity. It begins in a sacred marriage of opposites, the Earth or lunar goddess with the sun god. In many of these stories the bridegroom, the sun god, is sacrificed, killed, and then resurrects after three days. We must, in my opinion, be open to writing more revisionist stories today, just as the early writers of the gospels did. They did not take stories literally but wrote new stories that they knew were recycled from earlier ones. We do not have to get rid of the old stories we love. All we have to do is add a few new ones.

The new story that is coming into focus as we piece together newly found gospels and biblical scholarship has brought us the possibility that Mary Magdalene was a partner of Jesus, perhaps a lover and wife. In Aramaic, Magdala means, "tower," "watch-tower," and "fortress," so it may have been a nickname for a woman of towering strength. She was clearly a woman of towering strength who was perhaps Jesus' best student and closet friend. Jewish rabbis like Jesus were expected to marry, both in the ancient world and today. Excellent scholars have shared historical reasons that have convinced many of us that Jesus was married to Mary Magdalene. Dr. Karen King from Harvard and others have gifted us with translations and editorials of the *Gospel of Mary Magdalene*, a Gnostic gospel that represents Mary Magdalen as a leader and teacher in one of the early house-church communities. Dialogue in this Gospel expresses the jealousy that the male disciples may have had, and Peter says bitterly, "Did Jesus then, speak with a woman in private without our knowing it? Are we to turn around and listen to her? Did he choose her over us?" (Mary 10: 3-4). Perhaps you are, like me, a woman and recognize this familiar kind of misogynistic interaction. Power does not concede without a fight, as they say, and some men and women alike are not giving up old models of power-over relationships gracefully. Many in power are not welcoming those of us who have too often been left out.

Men with influence and maturity are people in a position to support women in religious leadership as John Cobb has supported me. We need the women now more than ever before. This is what Levi was doing in the Gospel of Mary as he defends Mary against Peter's assaults and celebrates her leadership.

> Peter, you have always been a wrathful person. Now I see you contending against the woman like the Adversaries. For if Jesus made Mary Magdalene worthy, who are you then for your part to reject her? Assuredly Jesus's knowledge of her is completely reliable. That is why he loved her more than us. Rather we should be ashamed. We should clothe ourselves with the Perfect Human, acquire it for ourselves, as Jesus commanded, and announce the good news, not laying down any other rule or law that differs from what Jesus said.[1]

We are also called to be in partnership with loving men like Levi, who defends and champions Mary Magdalene as Jesus had done.

So, you may ask, if she was so important to Jesus, why was Mary Magdalene left out? Perhaps for her own safety. After Jesus was crucified, if she was his wife and the mother of his child, as Margaret Starbird imagines, his followers may have wanted her to be taken to safety as a political refugee. Now the lost bride of our patriarchal religion is back to empower women into leadership. If

---

1. King, Karen L., *The Gospel of Mary of Magdala Jesus and the First Woman Apostle* (Santa Rosa, CA: Polebridge Press, 2003), 17–18.

she can do it, survive the trauma of her life and continue a life of teaching and preaching, then so can you and I.

May the spirit of Jesus and Mary Magdalene and the partnership model they represent become the model for the world. We need it now more than ever. It has survived two thousand years of being left out, lied about, and dishonored. You, the reader, are invited to go forth and embody that model. Regardless of the hardships ahead, God calls us to gather, men and women together. We are called to share how God is working in our lives, and to share the truth of what is happening in our world.

EARTH CRISIS SUPPORT GROUPS

Thank you, John Cobb, for being so honest with us in the previous chapters. Now, readers, it is your turn. I invite you to form small groups—what we are calling Earth Crisis Support Groups— where you can share your personal stories with each other. It is past time for people of all faiths and no faith to work together before we blow up ourselves and God's creation. This is the new kind of house-church we need to create—fast. Jesus was not a Christian; he was a Jew, and he invited everyone whether they were Jewish or not. We are called now to invite people to small settings to work together in effective ways. We will get to know one another by sharing truthfully about our lives and about how we feel. This is how we can be inspired, as the early Christians were, to change the world for love not war, for justice not domination, violence, and cruelty.

How do you learn to love your enemy? I believe now that it is a decision you make with God's help. We never condone the cruel, destructive behavior of ourselves or others, but we are called by God to work to understand it. We cannot love our enemies in other countries if we do not also do the inner work to learn how to love the enemies within us and in our own personal lives.

This is hard work. Rev. Dr. Martin Luther King had classes

in nonviolent disobedience where they practiced having people scream and harass them without responding back. Walter Wink, like John Cobb, relates the teachings of Jesus to our modern crisis in his small, highly recommended book, *Nonviolence and Jesus, A Third Way*. We are never to respond to violence or aggression with more violence and aggression. We are never to lie down and act like a doormat. We are called to find a third way, a more creative response that always has the conversion of our oppressor as part of our vision. We learn this best with other people in community.

Our very Mother, our common home, Mother Earth, seems to be coming up from under the earth and urging us to awaken. Many of us are slowly but surely waking up. We must do everything in our power to give birth to loving relationships of partnership with men and women working together to save our common home, Mother Earth. I feel a responsibility to my grandchildren to create a safe harbor for them to experience and learn from the natural world.

Suzanne Simard's brilliant new book, *Finding the Mother Tree*, is a confessional story. She coined the term Mother Tree to describe the oldest and largest trees in the forest. They are not female, per se; however, what they do is like what loving mothers do. The Mother Tree is in intimate relationship with all the living creatures in her community. She communicates with and is in life-giving relationship to a huge underground network of connections invisible to the human eye—just like love, prayers, and dreams connect us in ways we cannot see, or how the Internet is a worldwide web inviting nonlocal relationships. The Mother Tree has huge roots that go down as far as three hundred miles underground. She is in intimate relationship and communicates with both her own kin as well as other species. She does not stop healing and nurturing her community, even as she is failing in health, getting old, and is dying.

People are called today to pray with the trees and other creatures. Love is the key that unlocks the Secret Prayer Garden of our hearts. Healing is wrapped and interwoven in God's radical

love for our wellbeing, and we heal one another in the same way.
Love is miraculously powerful and regenerative. We are called to
go deep within our hearts and do this profound spiritual work of
learning to love in small groups. Maybe we as women don't have to
save Christian discipleship alone. Maybe S/he, our Mother Father
God and Mother Earth and Father Sky are trying to get our attention and connect us to the trees, animals, and ecosystems. May
we gather in small groups, eat, talk truthfully and pray together
and love one another. S/he will lead us where we need to go. As
Suzanne shares in *Finding the Mother Tree*, "Maybe we don't have
to save the trees, maybe they will save us." God, who is within every
living creature, is trying to get in touch with you. It is past time
for all of us in the human family to gather round the bedside of
Mother Earth, who really is our shared mother, and pray together.
As they say, everyone believes in God in the foxhole, and we, my
dear friend, are together today in a fox hole. You want to learn
how to pray? It is simple. Just talk to God, Her beloved creatures,
including Mother Earth, the trees, the soil and water, chickens,
whales, roses—all the creatures, galaxies, and stars.

Appendix

Guidelines for Earth Crisis Support Groups

T HERE ARE all sorts of small groups that help people deal with particular problems. But we know of none that help people to deal with the threat to human survival. We feel called to encourage the formation of such groups. Some may be composed of disciples of Jesus. Others of Muslims. Others of atheists. Others who are spiritual but not religious. And others, perhaps most, human beings of all stripes who want help in dealing with their partly suppressed fears.

Being with other people who have signed up to share their feelings and have committed to gather regularly to get to work in the world will empower us. Twelve-step programs have grown worldwide and effectively transform people's lives when people share the truth with themselves and others in groups that meet regularly. The early church began in people's homes as house churches.

Small groups of people gathered to tell the truth about what was going on in their lives and the world. Base communities in Latin America in the 1960s inspired revolutionary change for individuals and communities. Psychology groups and medical support groups have enabled people who were sick and in various stages of healing and recovery to form loving bonds. Even if a woman is dying from breast cancer, for example, if she has a breast cancer support group, she will have a vastly better and less lonely quality of life.

Women in the early church and today are often the people who create community by sharing a meal. There is incalculable spiritual nourishment gained when we share the truth of our lives in a safe place, with others who do the same—regularly and repeatedly. Food is the magic ingredient second only to what? The truth. These groups all share their personal truth about their shared circumstances. Because they know how hard it can be to tell the truth, they suspend judgement and send love to the other members. Telling the truth to one another is how we become close, and when we do it—we no longer feel so all alone.

This may seem like a little, but it is not. Truth telling is a big mountain of something. Everybody needs someone to talk to about what is going on in their lives. Sharing our feelings is not an end in itself. This is the first step to movement, change, and new adventures. There are two big mountains. One is telling the truth. The second mountain is going into the world and trying something new. New pathways in our brains are forged as we break through our denial. We discover new possibilities we never dreamed possible. We discover and create exciting new projects with others locally and globally. If and when we tell the truth with others, we crack open our denial and wake up. We begin the process of adventures and action in the world. We begin to explore creative solutions beyond what we imagined was possible.

We are living with a threat to human survival. This is the sixth extinction of life on Earth, the only one created by us humans.

Many of us are aware of the horrors of nuclear warfare, species extinction, famines and poverty, war, social and institutional collapse, and the rise of fascism. Our suicide rate is skyrocketing and depression and addiction are rampant. Many young people do not want to have children. Most of us have gone into denial because it is just too painful to face that we are living in the most existentially dangerous time, not only in human history but in the 4.5-billion-year history of our common home, our beloved Mother Earth.

This planetary crisis may seem to be the least of your problems if personal responsibilities are overwhelming you. Fortunately, or unfortunately, depending on how you want to look at it, we are an interconnected web of life—both with each other, as a human family, and with all the other creatures. On some level, all of us know instinctually that we are living in the most dangerous time in the history of our human and planetary family. We are all affected by this reality, whether we like it or not. However, there is something you can do today to respond in a more loving and conscious way for yourself, for other people, and for all life on planet Earth. Invite a small group of people for a potluck dinner, with the intention of sharing truthfully about your feelings, and tell the truth to yourself and one another about what is really going on at this historic time.

Denial, as they say, is not just a river in Egypt. It is a fantastically effective coping mechanism—which is why we use it. The problem with denial is that it not only shuts off our negative feelings, but it shuts off our life source, as well. Whether we are conscious or unconscious about global suffering, many of us act as if it is not happening and that everything is OK. This is a lie, and the truth will set us free. Why gather regularly with the intention to talk about the horrific truth? Because most of us do not have a person, family or small support group, tribe, network, or community where we can connect and be completely truthful about the state of the world. Feelings need to be expressed in a safe place or they get stuck inside us where, like a cancer, they grow and infect every aspect of our wellbeing. Having loving relationships is what enables humans to survive a crisis and come out the other end. Many feelings live underneath our awareness, and when we get in touch with these feelings, we are often shocked at their potential to lift us out of lethargy and despair. We fear that our feelings may destroy us, but, in reality, they are like healthy blood that, when it flows freely, enlivens our whole being—mind, body, and psychospiritually.

When we are with a safe person or safe small group of people, like a loving family that is committed to loving and supporting us when we are in crisis, we begin to feel better faster than if we have to survive our crisis alone. We know that the modern world has greatly diminished the health and power of the family unit to be a major source of love and support. If you don't have a family to love and support you during this planetary crisis, or your family has a habit of minimizing or ignoring the larger world, you can adopt a new family-like tribe or support group. If sharing your deepest feelings is foreign to you and something you don't do in your family, please be assured that many of us did not grow up sharing our feelings in our families but have learned late in life.

As we experiment and bravely share our feelings and the truth of our lives and the world, we begin to feel massively better. We may discover that some of our feelings, like anger, for example, may actually be covering up an array of different underlying feelings such as hurt and fear. We may not have any idea how we are feeling about our Earth crisis because we have never had a place to talk about them before. Many of us have had great sorrow and depression as we learned the extent of our Earth crisis. The good news is that we do not have to be alone in this journey. We learn fast how to explore and express our feelings if and when we are around others who are doing the same. Most of us just need an invitation to share truthfully in a safe place. It works. If I share deeply, others feel safe to follow and share deeply also. This happens naturally.

John Cobb and I are extending an invitation to you to begin a group for sharing the truth of our interconnected lives. Invite a small group of people to gather in order to talk about our Earth crisis, share feelings, and and brainstorm about how to respond effectively. The guidelines below are simple.

1. Gather in a small group of about 6–8 people, at least weekly. Read these guidelines out loud and make a group agreement to use them.

2. Go around the circle two separate times. The first time, share truthfully how you are feeling about your personal life, each person taking at least five minutes.

3. The second time, share truthfully how you are feeling about the threat to human survival, the potential for nuclear war, and our planetary ecological crisis, with each person taking about five minutes

4. Share a potluck meal, with conversation exploring creative responses to this crisis together and individually.

5. After dinner, everyone helps to clean up. Share any announcements and decide whose house or where you will meet for your gathering the following week.

One person is assigned the role of facilitator of each meeting who assigns a timekeeper and reads the following guidelines:

1. Everyone is invited to share without being interrupted.

2. No cross talk, meaning we do not comment on what other people have shared, and we refrain from interrupting people except to ask clarifying questions.

3. Everything shared in the group is kept in confidence with the group.

4. Assign a timekeeper to make sure everyone is given the same amount of time to share; about five minutes depending on how many people, longer as time permits.

5. Encourage "I" statements, "I feel—." If you do not know how you are feeling and have nothing to say, the group will sit in silence for your allotted time and wait. It is a gift to be together in silence. Silence is meaningful and you are invited to love everyone in the silences as well as in conversation.

6. When there is a conflict in any group, set aside a time solely for a discussion about the issue or conflict after your regular time together. All information about the issue is shared, and everyone is invited to speak about their ideas and feelings. Usually, a wiser group solution is revealed naturally in conversation. Earth Crisis Support Groups also have a committee of experienced group leaders who are available for consultation if necessary.

If we share a meal together, we feel closer to one another. Just like families who gather regularly to share a meal, we develop closer relationships when we eat and talk together. Sharing food and talking about our feelings, trying out new ideas with others and getting feedback, and processing possible actions we can take nourishes our spirits as surely as food nourishes our bodies. We will gain a sense of wellbeing when we go out into the world and get to work.

Passionate determination is the best medicine for what ails us today. Doing civil disobedience is empowering. Marching and singing is joyful. Being together is what matters. Together we can work to save our habitat for future generations of all species. We will become actualized human beings. When we tell the truth, we develop a sense of loving connection to one another. Including food is a key to community building that works. Enjoy your meal and conversation together after you have had your deep personal sharing.

That's it. Good luck! We may discover ways of acting in the world that will surprise us all. When we humans have a sense of purpose and meaning, our despair begins to dissolve. We do not have to be alone. We are in this together and sharing the truth together invites joy and laughter amidst the crisis. It is possible that your group will become inspired to read books, discuss ideas, develop programs, share spiritual practices, collaborate with others—there is no limit to the possibilities on how your group will evolve. There is no deeper spiritual practice and potential for creative genius than committing to loving relationships. Anyone and everyone is welcome and invited to these small support groups.

It is time to organize a living Earth movement with our human family around the world, one small group at a time, using our commitment to truth telling and close relationships to create loving communities. What else do we have to do that's more important than saving our Earth?

Printed in the USA
CPSIA information can be obtained
at www.ICGtesting.com
LVHW020844280124
770074LV00001B/243

9 781940 447600